Twayne's Filmmakers Series

Warren French
EDITOR

John Ford

John Ford. Courtesy of Museum of Modern Art.

John Ford

PETER STOWELL

Florida State University

BOSTON
Twayne Publishers
1986

John Ford

Peter Stowell

Copyright © 1986 by G. K. Hall & Co.
All Rights Reserved
Published by Twayne Publishers
A Division of G. K. Hall & Co.
70 Lincoln Street
Boston, Massachusetts 02111

Copyediting supervised by Lewis DeSimone
Book production by Lyda E. Kuth
Book design by Barbara Anderson

Typeset in 11 pt. Garamond
by Compset, Inc. of Beverly, Massachusetts

Printed on permanent/durable acid-free paper
and bound in the United States of America

Library of Congress Cataloging in Publication Data

Stowell, Peter.
John Ford.

(Twayne's filmmakers series)
Bibliography: p. 154
Includes index.
1. Ford, John, 1894–1973—Criticism and interpretation.
I. Title. II. Series.
PN1998.A3F6256   1986   791.43'0233'0924   85-24808
ISBN 0-8057-9305-4
ISBN 0-8057-9306-2 (pbk.)

*This book is dedicated to
Erin, Lex, and Rachel,
all of whom ride
tall in the saddle.*

Contents

About the Author

PETER STOWELL was born in Brockville, Ontario. He received his Ph.D. from the University of Washington in Comparative Literature. He was one of the founders of the Seattle Film Society and *Movietone News*. Currently, he teaches European literature and a number of film courses at Florida State University, and is Director of the Film Studies Program. In 1978 he was awarded The President's Teaching Award. He was one of the founders of the annual Comparative Literature Conference on Literature and Film at Florida State University. He has published *Literary Impressionism, James and Chekhov* and a number of articles on both literature and film. He has also consulted with McKinsey and Co. on the uses of feature films as an instrument for organizational change.

Editor's Foreword

THE CLAIM OF John Ford to a place in this series, or any other devoted to auteurist filmmakers scarcely needs further support; even the filling out of such a program would provide no adequate reason for simply another introduction to this much honored and studied director. Rather than providing a hurried survey of Ford's long career and many credits, Peter Stowell has chosen to concentrate on fourteen of Ford's talking pictures released over the three decades 1933 and 1962 in order to focus upon what Stowell considers Ford's most important contributions to the development of six of the most influential myths of the United States. What these are and how Ford has shaped them, Stowell explains in his preface.

There are precedents in this series for such an approach to an auteurist's work in Leland Poague's *Howard Hawks* and Gary Morris's *Roger Corman*. Ford, Hawks, and Corman have all been prolific filmmakers, frequently producing genre films that they have elevated from the level of routine stereotypes to visualized myths. Ford's and Hawks's visions of the frontier West have replaced in the minds of generations of filmgoers the historical West in much the way that John Milton's *Paradise Lost* replaced the stark story of Man's Fall in Genesis (and these, too, tell of a paradise lost). Corman has used Poe's tales as a springboard for a nihilistic vision of the modern world in a medium that would have enchanted Poe. A book about Ford's achievement was an urgent necessity to complement the Hawks and Corman books, and we are greatly pleased that Peter Stowell has provided exactly what was needed for one of the final volumes to bring this project to a triumphant conclusion.

W. F.

Preface

JOHN FORD, apart from being one of the world's greatest filmmakers, was one of America's great chroniclers and mythmakers. His position is unique, for not only are his films landmarks in the history of cinema, but they are also cultural artifacts that express America's deepest concerns, problems, and ideals. Except among film aficionados, Ford's works have entered a kind of cultural mainstream where they are vaguely recollected as aspects of America's real and mythical history. The medium for this mainstream is, of course, television, where Henry Fonda and John Wayne parade through American History on Sunday mornings, while John Ford is virtually forgotten. The major reason Ford is overlooked by the public when, say, Alfred Hitchcock and Orson Welles are not, is that Ford is cinema's consummate classical stylist. His stylistic restraint, unity of form and content, and apparent simplicity shift all attention to the films' stories. Yet it is this subtlety that draws filmmakers, critics, and scholars to Ford. The art of narrative filmmaking can be learned from him. And this is what Orson Welles meant when he said that he prepared for *Citizen Kane* by watching Ford's *Stagecoach* over forty times. Welles had no intention of imitating Ford's style. Instead, learning from Ford is to return to the master of classical Hollywood filmmaking. Though Ford may be forgotten, his stories are not. Directors as diverse as Federico Fellini, François Truffaut, Satyajit Ray, Jean Renoir, Hitchcock, and Welles have all noticed that one does not simply see a Ford film; instead, one completely enters and experiences the palpable smell and feel of a world rich in people, life, and images.

One feels both comfortable and uncomfortable these days using the phrase "a Ford film," because there are many ramifications of film theory involved in that simple phrase. It is not my intention to resolve these issues through a comprehensive debate, but rather briefly to put "auteurism," the problem of film authorship, into perspective. Ford is often at the center of this debate—witness the British Film Institute's reader, *Theories of Authorship*. The editor of this reader justifies using

Ford as the reader's prime auteur on this basis: "the choice of Ford was motivated by the fact that he seems to have figured in theory more continuously, more centrally, and more variously than any other director."[1]

My goal has been to establish the larger patterns in Ford's filmmaking career. Ford was one of those directors rarely satisfied with the extent of his control. In Hollywood there were basically three options for such directors. One alternative was to fight the studio system in an effort to create exactly the films one wanted. The usual result of such an approach was banishment from the monolithic, commercial system; Erich von Stroheim and Welles are prime examples. Another way was to deliberately prefer making "B" films, low-budget projects that played on the bottom half of double features. Here the likes of Edgar G. Ulmer and Jacques Tourneur worked in obscurity and relative freedom because the studios' financial risks were slight. The third possibility was that taken by Ford and Hitchcock. Through shrewdness, mental toughness, stubbornness, willingness to compromise, and commercial success these directors were able to navigate the shoals of "A" feature studio filmmaking. Regardless of which style this third group of pantheon directors chose, they have come to be known as "auteurs."

Too often those who have attacked the auteur theory for promoting individual self-expression at the expense of the collective production process have failed to acknowledge the extent to which authorship is in fact a give-and-take manipulation of the collective process. Any attempt to separate an auteur's desire for filmic self-expression from his desire for nuts-and-bolts involvement in and control over the collective process is naive and simplistic.

My book works on the assumptions that Ford *did* project his style, ideals, attitudes, and values onto the screen, that he *did* involve himself in and control as much of the on-screen production as possible, that he *did* whatever he could to insure an uninterrupted, lifelong career in commercial filmmaking, and that by any number of critical standards he *did* make and was largely responsible for a surprising number of superlative films that have either become international classics or have contributed to that body of American cultural artifacts known as Americana.

I have chosen those of Ford's films that I believe constitute the six most essential myths of the American dream. Together, these myths unify a major portion of Ford's work into a coherent vision of the American experience. The usual division and classification of these films is Westerns and Americana.[2] Each has established codes and conventions, particularly the Western, and each has strong mythical concerns and structures. They are typically described as genres. Certainly there is nothing wrong with analyzing much of Ford's canon in these terms.

However, I hope that by changing this pattern it will be possible to shift some of the emphasis on Ford away from his identity as a moviemaker to his identity as creator of cultural artifacts working in film. So, instead of a loosely conceived myriad of myths or the arbitrarily reductive and meaninglessly broad, say, "Myth of the West" or "Myth of America," I am proposing a more clearly delineated and ultimately more complete structure for Ford's Americana and Western films. I also believe that these films and this structure penetrate the heart of Ford's work as a whole. While many films and a number of other genres have not been discussed in this work, I am confident that even such films as those usually classified as Ford's "War," "Irish," or "Foreign" films could be effectively explicated by way of one or more of the myths of the American dream. Ford's controlling sensibility was American, no matter how Irish he tried to be. Besides, virtually all of these films were made by American studios for American audiences. The American dream was the most powerful metaphor for the American experience, all the way from a studio head to the audience the film was made for.

I have, therefore, identified what I believe to be the six essential myths that were central to John Ford's filmmaking consciousness, to the film industry in which and for which he worked, and to the American dream: the myth of the American Adam, the myth of the American frontier, the myth of the American democrat, the myth of American agrarianism, the myth of American individualism, and the myth of American civilization. These six myths of the American dream will serve as my structural model for Ford's American experience as expressed in fourteen of his films.

Though this book is about six American myths vis-à-vis the American dream, its emphasis is given over to the complex, realistic power of the myths. The American dream is the idealistic fantasy that generates the dilemmas posed by the positive and negative aspects of each myth's dialectical structure. For instance, in Ford's films the American dream is always played out on some kind of frontier. The frontier is always a place of struggle and mediation set as it must be on the ever-changing cusp between the positive and negative qualities of the wilderness and the positive and negative qualities of civilization. On the frontier the American dream avoids banality because it is tested and challenged in the crucible of change, struggle, and mediation. Ford and his screenwriters developed complex mythologies for a complex world, not the idealistic, nostalgic ones of a simplistic world, as has been charged in some quarters.

Ford stands firmly in the tradition of mythmakers who are both historians and storytellers and who believe as Ford did that "you build a legend and it becomes a fact."[3] Mythmakers use history to make history. They want to help shape the world in which they live. In Ford's films the relationship of history to myth is dialectical, dynamic, and controversial. I believe that Ford used film to mediate between recorded history and mythical history, so that while the tension and play between them remain, history has become myth and myth history through film. This makes Ford's pictures more than simply entertainment and more, even, than self-expression. They have been drawn from the depths of America's cultural, political, historical, and mythological wellspring and have become important interpretations of that wellspring. Certainly Ford's films are important to the history of cinema and the American entertainment industry. His films have influenced the way succeeding filmmakers have made films and many of his films have been critical and commercial successes. Ford himself was influential within the industry.

Ford's vision is important not because it is personal but because it is communal, and Ford's films are not great because they tell deeply embedded mythical histories but because he knew how to tell these stories in the medium he had chosen. So, it is not enough for me to identify what I believe to be the mythical constructs that Ford's films express, but I must also describe how he is able to express them. To this end I will proceed through close analysis of the mise-en-scène. Any study that takes as its central concern the mythic patterns of a culture or nation in one of its artists must to a large extent be a thematic, content-oriented study. However, since I firmly believe that what is expressed is inseparable from how it is expressed, I hope to avoid auteur reductiveness, thematic literariness, and cultural oversimplification by concentrating on the specificity of the medium's means of expression, particularly mise-en-scène and cinematographic properties. For instance, if it is possible to identify certain patterns in the mise-en-scène of, say, the films of American Agrarianism, then it is possible to generalize about their content. I am not solely interested in the mythic structures I have identified as important to Ford's films. Instead, I think it is just as crucial to discover how each film's and group of films' mythic discourse is developed, articulated, and insured. In this way, the meaning that is read into the film finds its source in how it is expressed, thereby avoiding hollow, disembodied statements of content. Ford, then, becomes more than a mere conveyor of mythic tales; he stands, instead, as a practitioner in the art of mythmaking.

In an effort to confirm the extent of Ford's and his screenwriters' mythmaking abilities, to further explore the nature and style of their storytelling, to make a final case for romance as the dominant genre in Ford's canon, and to demonstrate both the continuity and the changes in Ford's filmmaking career, I have included a chapter on narrative structure. A graphic representation of the diachronic (horizontally, across time) and the synchronic (vertically, within the same moment in time) narrative structures of *Stagecoach* and *The Searchers* should reveal a number of elements in Ford's films that were not possible to express in the expository chapters on mythic structures. Narratology has proven to be a crucial link in the quest toward an understanding of myths and mythmaking. Through a study of two narratives I hope to reinforce the auteur-structuralist thrust of this book, temporarily to redirect the book's emphasis away from mise-en-scène, cinematographic properties, and dialogue, and to demonstrate more fully the component parts of romance.

I believe that both Ford's American films and his Westerns are joined together in content by quests for the American dream and that such quests take the generic form of romance. Northrop Frye, in his influential work on literary classification, began the essay on romance with the statement that the "romance is nearest of all literary forms to the wish-fulfillment dream."[4] And no dream is more wish-fulfilling than the American dream. This kind of approach has been used before, most notably in Frank McConnell's work *Storytelling and Mythmaking*. He sees a relationship between romance and war films (a major Ford genre) and Western's. He says, for instance, that "more than any other genre of American film—or any tradition of film—the Western reduplicates the possibilities and the abiding concerns of romance."[5]

It was Nathaniel Hawthorne who characterized romance as a mingling of the real and the marvelous. In the quest-adventure structure of their narratives and the dialectical structure of their characterizations Ford's films find their elements of the "marvelous." And in the meticulously authentic constructions of mise-en-scène his films become "real." Though his stories may be about the entropy of civilization and the violence of the wilderness and his characterizations about the exaltation of the hero through his perilous journeys and struggles with the wasteland, nevertheless, the feel, look, atmosphere, and details of what one actually sees within the boundaries of any one frame of a Ford film are simply and uncannily real. The quests and heroes are of this world. Romance is the form that allows all of Ford's attitudes and values concerning life and filmmaking to find expression.

If all of this seems, perhaps, too reductive, that is, that romance is the one generic form in which the content of Ford's overarching American vision is expressed, then one must acknowledge that this is one of the risks of criticism that attempts to illuminate through structure and classification. I am sensitive to this issue and have tried whenever possible to recognize that each film is an entity in itself with its own individual qualities and that each is filled with multitudes of play within its parts. I am also aware that Ford, like any creator who works over a period of time, changes, and that to impose a structure on his career is to suggest that he made films within a set of unchanging precepts. In an effort to counteract this inevitable impression I have analyzed the films in essentially a chronological order, while still grouping them under my six myths of the American dream. Then my chapter on narrative structure is an effort to treat two films from different eras in Ford's career, his middle and late periods, and to compare and contrast them on the basis of their diachronic and synchronic narrative structures. Through this approach I hope to show both the changes and the continuity in Ford's storytelling and filmmaking. And though I have chosen a particular method on which to hang this analysis, I want it to demonstrate some of the play within each film both between different sequences and between different levels within each sequence.

Ford was one of cinema's most playful and self-referential directors. His films are a joy to watch, his in-jokes are fun to recognize, and the connections between his films are intriguing to make. I hope that within the framework of an essentially scholarly work I have also conveyed the sheer pleasure of looking more deeply into the films of John Ford.

I would like to acknowledge the many students who have participated in a variety of John Ford courses and contributed to my understanding of his films; Fred Standley, who generously allowed flexible teaching schedules; the Florida State University Foundation for a grant to study Ford's silent films; Howard Mandelbaum at Phototeque and Charles Silver and Mary Corliss at the Museum of Modern Art for their help with silent films and stills; Diana Bourdon and Daphne Liedy for intelligent editing and typing; Warren French for firm, intelligent editing; Wolf and Winnie Adolph for stimulating coffee breaks and valuable suggestions; Fred Silva, a kindred spirit and great influence; and Anne for eternal support.

PETER STOWELL

Florida State University

Chronology

1895	John Augustine Feeney, Jr. born in Cape Elizabeth, Maine, on 1 February.
1912– 1914	Plays football for Portland High; nicknamed "Bull" Feeney, the human battering ram.
1914	Graduates from high school; ready to attend University of Maine. Enter long-lost older brother, Francis, now a Hollywood actor-director, known as Francis Ford. John Feeney, Jr. goes to Hollywood to work with his brother. Takes the name Jack Ford.
1914– 1917	Works with Francis as jack-of-all-trades, including propman, stuntman, actor, and assistant director.
1917	Directs first film for Carl Laemmle and Universal–101 Bison, *The Tornado*, a two-reeler. Also directs first feature-length film, *Straight Shooting*.
1917– 1921	Teams with Western star Harry Carey to make twenty-four films.
1920	Marries Mary McBride Smith, 3 July.
1921	Makes first trip to Ireland, and his ancestral home, Galway.
1921– 1931	Works exclusively for Fox Films.
1920– 1935	Works with the great cameraman George Schneiderman on twenty-two films.
1923	Changes his professional name from Jack to John Ford, for his first big Fox picture, *Cameo Kirby*.
1924	First major success, and the most important Western of its time, *The Iron Horse*.
1926	Finest silent film, *Three Bad Men*.

1927   Goes to Germany to shoot background scenes for *Four Sons*; meets great Expressionist director, F. W. Murnau.

1929   First talking feature, *The Black Watch*.

1930   Beginning of a thirteen-film collaboration with screenwriter Dudley Nichols, *Men without Women*.

1931   *Arrowsmith*, first picture in a decade away from Fox.

1933   Directs the first of three films with Will Rogers, *Dr. Bull* (other two: *Judge Priest*, 1934, and *Steamboat Round the Bend*, 1935).

1934   Buys his most prized possession, the *Araner*, a 110-foot ketch. *The Lost Patrol*.

1935   Directs three films in different styles for different studios: *The Whole Town's Talking*, *The Informer*, *Steamboat Round the Bend*. Wins first Academy Award and New York Film Critics Award for Best Direction, for *The Informer*. *The Informer* wins New York Film Critics Award for Best Motion Picture.

1935   Will Rogers killed in plane crash.

1936   Directs first film for Darryl Zanuck at Twentieth Century-Fox, *The Prisoner of Shark Island*. Beginning of a ten-film collaboration with Zanuck. *Mary of Scotland*, *The Plough and the Stars*.

1937   *Wee Willie Winkie*, *The Hurricane*.

1938   *Four Men and a Prayer*, *Submarine Patrol*.

1939   Directs three classics: *Stagecoach*, *Young Mr. Lincoln*, and *Drums along the Mowhawk*. Wins New York Film Critics Award for Best Direction of *Stagecoach*. *Stagecoach* revitalizes the Western and launches John Wayne's career. *Young Mr. Lincoln* begins a seven-film collaboration with Henry Fonda.

1939–   Makes unofficial intelligence expeditions on the *Araner* for
1941   the Navy.

1940   Wins Academy Award and New York Film Critics Award for Best Direction, for *The Grapes of Wrath*. Also directs *The Long Voyage Home* from Eugene O'Neill plays.

1941   Wins Academy Award and New York Film Critics Award for Best Direction, for *How Green Was My Valley*. That film also won Academy Award for Best Film. Directs *Tobacco Road*.

1941   Promoted to Commander John Ford, U.S.N.R. on 11 September. Put in charge of the Field Photographic Branch. Pearl Harbor, 7 December.

1942   June: films the Battle of Midway from a control tower. September: America's first war documentary, *The Battle of Midway*, is released. Wins an Academy Award for Best Documentary.

1943   *December 7th*, a potentially explosive documentary on the attack of Pearl Harbor. Shot principally by Gregg Toland, but suppressed by the Navy. Released in a tepid form by Ford. Wins 1944 Oscar for Best Documentary.

1945   Awarded the Legion of Merit. *They Were Expendable*.

1946   Directs last film for Zanuck, *My Darling Clementine*. Then, with Merian C. Cooper, forms Argosy Productions.

1947   Argosy's first production, *The Fugitive*, based on the Graham Greene novel, *The Power and the Glory*, is an unmitigated disaster. Ford's last film with Dudley Nichols.

1948   Begins the long, eleven-picture collaboration with screenwriter Frank Nugent. Their first film is also the start of Ford's "cavalry trilogy," *Fort Apache* (other two: *She Wore a Yellow Ribbon*, 1949, and *Rio Grande*, 1950). Directs *Three Godfathers*.

1950   The beginning of the three-film John Wayne–Maureen O'Hara team, *Rio Grande*. Directs *Wagonmaster*, and *When Willie Comes Marching Home*.

1952   Greatest personal success, *The Quiet Man*. Wins his fourth and final Academy Award for Best Direction. Also Argosy Productions's last film. Directs unsuccessful remake of *What Price Glory?*

1953   Exhausting African trek for *Mogambo*. Has cataracts removed. Francis Ford dies, 6 September.

1954   *The Sun Shines Bright* (remake of *Judge Priest*).

1955   *The Long Gray Line*. *Mister Roberts*. Suffers gall bladder attack; Mervyn LeRoy finishes film.

1956   Reunited with Cooper for what is usually considered Ford's greatest film, *The Searchers*.

1957   *The Wings of Eagles*, *The Rising of the Moon*.

1958   *The Last Hurrah*.

1959   *The Horse Soldiers*, *Gideon of Scotland Yard*, *Korea* (documentary).

1960   *Sergeant Rutledge*.

1961   *Two Rode Together*.

1962   Last great film, *The Man Who Shot Liberty Valance*.

1963   *Donovan's Reef*. Participation *How the West Was Won* with Henry Hathaway and George Marshall.

1964   *Cheyenne Autumn*.

1965   *Young Cassidy*, a Ford project, but illness forces him off the film. Completed by Jack Cardiff.

1966   Final film, *7 Women*.

1967–1972   Works on a variety of projects, most of a historical nature, all unrealized.

1973   Receives the American Film Institute's first Life Achievement Award. President Richard M. Nixon presents Ford with the nation's highest civilian honor, the Medal of Freedom, 31 March (televised on 2 April). Dies 31 August, in Palm Springs.

1

The Myth of the American Adam: Will Rogers

JOHN FORD knew about frontiers. He had grown up in one, Portland, Maine, an outpost of the cradle of American civilization; went to live in another, California, America's last mythic frontier; and went to work in a third, the movies. A militant individualist and man of action in a pioneer industry, he played his role to the hilt by making his name in Westerns and hanging out with broncbusters, ranch hands, and stuntmen. During his teens and twenties he was working toward mythic interpretations of frontier America. But he needed a pioneer hero of real stature, an innocent man for a new land. It wasn't until 1932 when he met Will Rogers, who by that time was already a legendary figure, that he found his real mythic persona. He didn't need to manufacture him, either. Rogers gave Ford the opportunity to work with and work out a mythic figure on-screen. For a brief period Rogers was both a spokesman for and filmic expression of Ford's and America's frontier yearnings. He was the Indian summer of America's frontier dream.

It is not quite accurate to say, as Andrew Sarris did, that Rogers was the "major *auteur*" of his films with Ford.[1] It is true that in 1933, the year of their first film together, *Dr. Bull*, Rogers was a national institution, the best-loved man in the land, and Fox's second most-bankable movie star (Shirley Temple was first). Ford and Rogers were kindred spirits. The films they made were neither Roger's nor Ford's; they were Ford-Rogers films. Rogers, the man, simply was the American Adam, around whom Ford would provide the mythic story, setting, and resonances in a new medium. Rogers needed no heightened cinematic rhetoric to establish his mythic dimensions on-screen. So, instead of the usual low-angle introduction, dramatic musical flourish, rumored greatness, or mythic location, Ford slipped Rogers into each film with an almost comically low-keyed, casual entrance.

The Adamic myth has been a more powerful force in the American consciousness than the Edenic myth. In the beginning America was seen as the New Eden. But the Edenic myth lacked dynamic center. It was a stagnant, doomed place. But Adam is human, capable of being reborn, and has a mission to keep his innocence alive despite the ma-

chine, civilization, and evil. According to the original myth of the New
Eden and the New Adam, European culture lay in ruins, as Rousseau
had predicted, the victim of decadent overcivilizing. So the questers,
oppressed workers, religious outsiders, and the dispossessed of Europe looked to the New Promised Land. America conformed to the
pastoral ideal and the new inhabitants identified with Adam. So the
first polarity in American culture inevitably set European decadence
against American innocence. But, inevitably, this myth in the New
Land failed, too. For as R. W. B. Lewis notes in his influential study,
The American Adam, "The dangers, both to life and letters, of the
Adamic ideal were acknowledged at once and have been repeated endlessly. The helplessness of mere innocence . . . the dismissal of the
past" leads to tragedy.[2]

The American Adam moved west. It was in the West that he seemed
to have the freedom, space, spirit of equality, and opportunity to become truly the American Adam, not an eastern and warmed-over European model. This is the Adam that stuck, because he was more
completely American and because he was the last Adam. It was Will
Rogers, part-Indian from the West, who became America's most authentic and last Adam. Mass communication allowed Rogers to become
the only Adam to present himself as he was. He spoke to Americans
over the radio, wrote to them in the newspapers, roped for them on
stage, and acted for them in the movies. Whatever the medium, he
was always himself. Everything about Will Rogers signified emergence, freshness, and innocence. But he also embodied the contradictions of polarity. He was a mediator. He was the uncommon common
man, the eternal boy with the wisdom of the ages, the skeptical opti-
mist, the natural man who charmed the sophisticates, the folk philosopher who manipulated the media, the friend to every man with a
deep reservoir of loneliness. Both white and Cherokee from the prai-
ries of Oklahoma, this man of the West was born to mediate: he was
raised on a reservation, but not dependent on government funds (his
father ran a successful trading post); he had just enough, yet not too
much education, so that he could both take advantage of it and disre-
gard it; he brought his western rodeo tricks to eastern audiences; he
was a wanderer with a strong feeling for family and home; he believed
in progress and traditional values; his comedy was serious, though he
took nothing too seriously. His rumpled clothes, boyish grin, aw-
shucks manner, and imperfect grammar cemented America's dreams
and realities. He made people smile during the Depression, gave them
faith in their youthful energy, got them to laugh at themselves, taught
them to take nothing for granted, coached them in the joys of the vernacular, and, as a democratic Democrat, even enchanted the Republican money barons. He wielded power without making it seem sordid.

He was not a movie star, only good ol' Will Rogers who made movies. He was America's last authentic hero. He lived during America's entry into the technological and information age. He used the technology, but was not sullied by it. He did not become a hero through the always-tainted heroism of war. He expressed America's most positive values. He was just innocent enough to express them sincerely and just wry and sly enough not to make people gag on them. John Wayne could never quite be Will Rogers's successor; Wayne's legend was built solely on a screen persona. His offscreen personality lacked wit, wisdom, and cultural cohesiveness. American heroes must fit the requirements of the romance: their public and private persona must be as one; they must be real and marvelous. Anything else is either too mundane or too fanciful. Americans want more than fictional heroes. So Will Rogers emerged from the nowhere of the American plains (the wilderness), a self-reliant wanderer who intuitively personified the American dream's mythical qualities of the American Adam, the American frontier, the American individualist, and the American democrat. He felt no need to carry the past with him nor the trappings of civilized grammar, diction, or clothing. He created his own language, history, and self. Wherever he went he embodied the goodness of those American values that were under siege.

Ford's three Will Rogers films depict a gradual progression from a pessimism over Eden's despoliation to an optimism based on the belief that Eden once existed and may again. Their first film, *Dr. Bull* (1933), based on James Gould Cozzens's novel *The Last Adam* (hence, the conscious working out of the Adamic myth), shows a craven and technological society attempting to undermine the innocent naturalness of its town doctor. The second, *Judge Priest* (1934), has a visual Edenic setting, but the natural Adam is imbued with the melancholy loss of his Eden. Finally, in *Steamboat Round the Bend* (1935) Ford and Rogers nostalgically celebrated the pastoral Eden in a playful, innocent romp. In each case, though, Will Rogers as Adam triumphs over his environment. Eden may be corrupt, lost, or trivial, but Adam retains his values of innocence and presentness.

Dr. Bull (1933)

Ford began Rogers's Adamic progression toward Eden in stark contrast to the final two films. Dr. Bull's contemporary New England, anti-Edenic setting is reinforced by dark winter light and confined spaces. While its frigid, flat frontal mise-en-scène has made this an unpopular film, its style fits its content. Even in 1933 with the beloved Will Rogers in his film, Ford was willing to create an unattractive visual correlative for his underlying thematic concerns. *Dr. Bull* becomes, then, the father of such equally dark and confined films as *Tobacco Road*, *The Sun Shines Bright*, *The Last Hurrah*, and *The Man Who Shot Liberty Valance*, all of which have been pilloried because they lack spacious beauty, depict a trivialized world, and celebrate diminished, aging heroes. They are the anachronistic American Adams that time and civilization have passed by. Their manner is straightforward, their methods uncompromising, and their powers diminished. They were neither the heroes nor a vision of the world audiences wanted to believe in or see.

Dr. Bull is locked in a bitter struggle against the powerful forces of civilization's bigotry, ignorance, and snobbery. He is a physician attempting to civilize through healing, but to the "civilized" citizenry he is an anachronistic boor. With irreverent glee and unconcerned individualism Dr. Bull tells people what he thinks, sings too loudly and off-key in the church choir, makes jokes at the cemetery, neglects table manners, complains about his work, ridicules the town hypochondriac, tells gossips to mind their own business, and refuses to knuckle under to the community leaders. His pleasures are the innocent and simple ones: singing with boyish spontaneity, knowing all the town's children, spending an evening by the fire with Janet Carmaker (Vera Allen) and homemade cider, delivering the child of a humble Italian family, searching for a cure for paralysis, and aiding teenagers in love. He tries to bring life to this dying world.

Ford's narrative approach to *Dr. Bull* was typical of his emerging style. First he allows Doc Bull's character to evolve naturally through his interaction with the community, then Ford develops situations of dialectical conflict. It is through these conflicts that the thematic and mythic dimensions occur. Bull's values come into sharp relief when he chooses to deliver the child of a working-class family rather than attend to a dying girl who works for the upper classes. And he exhibits no guilt when he is rebuked for letting the girl die. Instead he delivers a Darwinian salvo to the upper crust: "You either have the stamina to hang on and develop a resistance to this disease or you haven't got it." Later, after he accuses the bastion of industrial civilization, Herbert Banning (Berton Churchill), of polluting the town's water supply, Banning's response sets the machine against the garden: "We know your attitude toward modern improvements. Dr. Bull would have us riding around in a horse and buggy, if he had his way." In the end Dr. Bull is proven right—a typhoid epidemic spreads through town carried by Banning's polluted water. By that time Banning is accusing Bull of not curing the typhoid. The machine destroys the garden, then drives the last Adam out.

After his confrontation with Banning, Doc Bull walks out into the street where he encounters the bright, new luxury car of a young, modern diagnostician from the city. Doc Bull's old jalopy is parked right across the street for maximum impact. He stops for a moment, poised between the symbol of modern civilization and his own "horse and buggy." Poignantly, his shoulders droop (Ford at these moments usually shoots from behind his characters) as he feels the material weight of his failures. Then he shrugs his shoulders, accepting his choices, and proceeds to his own car. This young diagnostician is important because he more than anyone else personifies the difficult choices embodied in the march of civilization.

In order to find a cure for the paralysis of one of his patients Dr. Bull seeks the advice of this young doctor. When he arrives, he is ushered through an elaborate laboratory. A tracking shot places the machinery between camera and an admiring yet bemused Doc Bull. The young doctor with his clipped mustache, slicked-down hair, sterile white coat, and abrupt manner is Ford's paragon of pompous professionalism. During their interview a manifest opposition emerges between the old and the new, the town and the city, the general practitioner and the specialist, the country bumpkin and the urban sophisticate. Doc Bull jokes about the equipment, "With an exhibit like this you ought to have taken it to the Century of Progress." And, "if machinery will do you any good, you ought to keep people livin' for a hundred years." The young specialist is condescendingly amused by Dr. Bull's folk methods. He scoffs at all old ideas and places his faith in modern machinery, whereas Dr. Bull is more open to new ideas, though more ambivalent about the wonders of technology. It turns out, of course, that Aunt Myra's nose was as accurate as the lab's machinery in diagnosing the typhus and that Doc Bull's hunch was better than the medical foundation's tests in finding a cure for the paralysis. Neither Dr. Bull nor John Ford are opposed to progress—Doc Bull's search for a new serum is proof of that—but they are opposed to the dehumanized pomposity that civilization seems to engender.

The young doctor and his machinery represent the dehumanization in "progress." The telephone, however, is civilization's neutral object. The hub of the town is the telephone switchboard that functions as the film's structuring device, both as a source of narrative information and scene transitions. It is also, on the one hand, the communications network for civilization's useless and destructive gossip and, on the other, the transmitter of urgent calls for Doc Bull's services.

When Dr. Bull is finally dismissed from this failed Eden, Ford, a confessed admirer of democracy, has him *voted* out. Ford was always intrigued by the dangers of inherently good ideas. *Dr. Bull* is one of his earliest hard looks at progress and democracy. The democratic rules of the legendary town meeting are scrupulously observed: Janet Car-

maker is allowed to speak when the majority is reminded of her right
to do so and Doc Bull is allowed to defend himself; still he is voted out
of office. For Ford, democracy can only be tested and preserved when
through its orderly process it fails to produce the right result. Doc Bull
is an anachronism, the last Adam. Eden has disappeared, and the
townspeople don't want an Adam around to remind them of the loss of
their pastoral ideal. In *Dr. Bull* Ford gave us his first real glimpse into
the attitudes that would dominate his postwar films.

Judge Priest (1934)

In *Judge Priest*, in the warm dusk of the Old South, the pastoral
ideal is at least seen. This is the transitional film set between the ir-
revocably lost Eden and cast-out Adam of *Dr. Bull* and the nostalgically
unified Eden and Adam of *Steamboat Round the Bend*. *Judge Priest* is
the finest of these three films because it takes advantage of the tensions
and crosscurrents inherent in its middle position. As a judge, Will Rogers is situated perfectly in a mediating role. Many of the same mediating themes and motifs of this film will reappear in films of men who
also hold essential public positions, such as *Young Mr. Lincoln, My
Darling Clementine, She Wore a Yellow Ribbon, The Sun Shines
Bright, The Last Hurrah*, and *The Man Who Shot Liberty Valance*.

From Irvin S. Cobb's stories about a Judge Priest, Ford and his
screenwriters, Dudley Nichols and Lamar Trotti, extracted the film's
tragiccomic style and the judge's mythic dimension. This prologue addresses the tragedies and the comedies of the War Between the States
that have "haunted every grown man's mind." It continues by describing a fictitious Judge Priest who "seemed typical of the tolerance of
that day and the wisdom of that almost vanished generation." These
lines remind us of that lost Eden, Dr. Bull's contemporary New England town.

The opening scene establishes the basic conflict: Jeff Poindexter
(Stepin Fetchit), the chicken-stealing, innocent child of nature, is
being prosecuted by Senator Horace K. Maydew (Berton Churchill),
the pompous preserver of a bigoted civilization. Maydew's argument
is that Jeff is "a confirmed chicken thief" who "has no place in this
God-fearing community" and "who cometh from no man knows
whence." This is, of course, thinly veiled racism. During this bombast
Judge Priest reads the comics while the defendant sleeps on the bench.
Jeff and the judge are kindred spirits. The film refuses to show Judge
Priest making a judgment. Instead, the courtroom scene dissolves into
a shot of the judge and Jeff walking toward their Edenic fishing hole.
The message of this narrative gap is that Judge Priest's mediating pow-
ers are somehow magic and that Eden still exists—though it is being

invaded. The courtroom, with its confined space, railings that cut people off from one another, and rigid institutionalization, represents civilization, while the road to the fishing hole has depth, openness, and all the elements associated with that archetypal image of America's great pastoral scene—"gone fishin'." The lap dissolve and the unusual use of (in the early 1930s) lap voice-over confirm Judge Priest's magical mediating powers, as though he simply transports Jeff and himself out of the jaws of a definitive legal judgment. Jeff's mumbling voice becomes the link between the two worlds. The judgment of this "trial" is resolved in the same manner as the one at the end of the film, through a consensus brought about by a celebration of American small-town rituals.

Judge Priest's verdicts go to the heart of what Ford continually showed to be the essence of justice, upholding the spirit rather than the letter of the law. The judge puts it in his own colorful way; "Maybe I did have a hankerin' for the spirit of the law and not the letter. But as far as I know no one had cause to complain—'til now." In film after film Ford demonstrated that the march of civilization is epitomized by tensions engendered in the spirit versus the letter of the law. Mediators are needed to bring the two into harmony. Finally, the accused man is acquitted by a tidal wave of Civil War heroics and memories. The wave breaks on the well-timed playing of "Dixie." Eden has been momentarily preserved.

This Eden is like Leo Marx's "middle state" or "middle landscape" which existed "between two garden metaphors: a wild, primitive, prelapsarian Eden . . . and a cultivated garden embracing values not unlike those represented by the classic Virgilian pasture."[3] In Ford's films this "middle state" encompasses the wilderness and the garden, nature and civilization, equality and class. One scene in particular illustrates Ford's handling of these polarities. Quite early in the film Judge Priest's nephew, Rome (Tom Brown), returns home from law school in the North. Rome and his old girlfriend, Ellie May (Anita Louise), the wronged and supposedly fatherless girl, are not speaking. Since she lives next door, the judge makes sure a errant croquet ball lands in her yard so that he can ask Rome to fetch it. While they are waiting for Rome to return the ball, Judge Priest becomes so enraptured over his speech about the joys of young love that he fails to hear Jeff warning him that a goat is eating his precious mint leaves. Since mint is essential to his beloved juleps, he shoos the goat out the gate past a flock of freely roaming chickens. Just then Rome's mother, Judge Priest's sister, Carrie (Brenda Fowler), enters the gate and protests that the judge is encouraging an undesirable match between Rome and "*that* girl." She proceeds to lecture him on the undignified image he is presenting, that of a Circuit Court judge drinking mint juleps. "Dignity?" he replies, "I don't believe the Priest family will ever have to worry about dignity as long as you're alive and kickin'." When his sister says that "the name of Priest means something in Kentucky," he retorts, "Well, I've never heard that it meant intolerance." The goat and chickens roaming through town and the carefully tended mint patch and croquet lawn represent the merger of the wilderness and the garden. And when Judge Priest shoos the wilderness out of the garden, it is immediately replaced by his sister, that bastion of civilization.

Just as the judge sits on the bench to mediate society's conflicts, so now he sits on the steps of his home to mediate this family conflict. Ford physically situates him between the purveyor of civilization and the children of nature. Though we know where Judge Priest's values lie, he never forces them upon anyone. Instead, he governs through consensus, good sense, humor, and tolerance. His values and goals are vindicated: the accused murderer is acquitted, while Rome and Ellie May cement the bonds of true love.

Parades and dances are Ford's rituals of community cohesion. All but the scoundrels participate. Those who are most critical of Ford's films find these surges of emotional participation particularly hard to swallow. For these critics Ford's consensus finales are no more than corny happy endings tacked on to reinforce America's, Hollywood's, and John Ford's Pollyanna complex. However, American cinema has had so many happy-ending afterthoughts that one can clearly see the organic cohesion of Ford's finales. They are simply the natural culminations of the mediators' success. Those who join in at the end are participating in the great American melting-pot ideal. The final shot of *Judge Priest* has the parade sweep past and envelop the camera, clearly inviting the audience to participate in the ground swell of consensus. The two pompous and overbearing elitists, however, are not participants. The judge's sister is nowhere to be seen, while Senator Maydew stands to one side and politics. Whereupon, Francis Ford, in one of his classic, oft-to-be-repeated gestures of contempt for pomposity, spits a wad of tobacco juice into the senator's black silk top hat.

In *Steamboat Round the Bend* Will Rogers's American Adam will be fully integrated and in easy harmony with himself, nature, and the community. But in *Judge Priest* the factors of societal mediation are more complex, so the hero must reach deeper into the recesses of his solitary self. The American Adam has been touched by the lonely tragedies that befall Eden. In *Judge Priest* the tragedy of the Civil War has marked the community, whereas in *Steamboat* it will barely touch their lives. For Judge Priest the death of his wife and children during the war intensifies his alienation. Yet, at the same time, this allows him to be one with an entire community of Civil War survivors.

The scene in which the judge expresses his loneliness is one of

Judge Priest (Will Rogers) mediating. Courtesy of Phototeque.

Ford's most moving scenes. It is framed by and mingled with the blos-
soming romance of Rome and Ellie May, thereby throwing into greater
relief the judge's loss of his young wife and children. Rome, Jeff, and
the judge sit on the front porch listening to a whippoorwill, as soft
violins enhance the mood. The judge sits back with his feet on the rail
in that graceful, laid-back gesture Ford will come to evoke as the quin-
tessentially American pose. Judge Priest, with glasses on and pipe in
hand, is the image of the thoughtful observer of life and nature. "Listen
to that ol' whippoorwill calling his mate. Him and his kin been nestin'
around here for nigh on thirty years." Rome understands: "It's a lonesome kind of sound, isn't it, Uncle Billy?" "Umm. 'Tis so," responds
the judge. "You know, the good Lord never meant for nobody, man
nor bird, to live by theirselves." This brief exchange encompasses the
judge's past tragedy and loneliness as well as Rome's puppy-love pangs
of loss. Rome then asks the judge why he didn't come to live with his
family after his wife died. The judge, of course, jokes that he couldn't
stand his sister's cooking. But the unstated truth is that Judge Priest
needed his solitude, that it was necessary for him to preserve his memories, gain wisdom, and become the community's mediator. Loneliness
is an essential ingredient of the mythic hero.

Later, when the judge goes up to his bedroom, the music shifts from
Jeff's playing of "My Old Kentucky Home" to a sad, violin lyric. From

his upstairs window the judge takes one last look at Rome and Ellie May. The lonely violin lyric unobtrusively slides into a tune from his youth, "Just a Song at Twilight." He looks out the window again, and through the mists of the past he sees himself in his Confederate uniform with his young wife. He lights a candle, illuminating the portrait of his wife and two young children. Then, with a slight quaver in his throat, he turns his back to the camera and says, "It's been a long time, honey, since you and the babies went away." He continues to address her portrait as though she were a living presence. He tells her that their son would have been the same age as Rome, and that his homecoming is "what made it seem more lonesome than ever around here." He suddenly stops undressing, prepares to blow out the candle, and for an instant we see his face reflected in the portrait's glass, thus superimposed on mother and children. In one of Ford's most splendid privileged moments a family has been reunited by light, spirit, and cinema. Though it is a moment drenched in emotion and sentiment, Ford, true to his principle of distancing, refused to indulge in a facial close-up. And, when the judge does turn toward that portrait, we see him only in profile through a medium long shot. In the future Ford will use this device of the superimposed reflected image for some of his most important privileged moments.

Steamboat Round the Bend (1935)

In *Steamboat Round the Bend* Will Rogers, as Dr. John Pearly, snake-oil hawker and riverboat captain, is firmly ensconced in Eden. Like Huck Finn, he is a child (though much older) of nature who gains his strength from the river and lives by his wits. The town is less in evidence, the world more innocent, and Roger's position less prominent in this last film of the Will Rogers trilogy. The world of *Steamboat*, though basically set in the same period and location as *Judge Priest*, has not been touched by the same tensions and insidious figures of civilization. There is no pompous politician, no snooty sister, and no town bully. The Civil War is no longer a tragic event or even a subject for argument. Instead, *Steamboat* projects the image of Edenic timelessness, the river serving as the metaphor for eternal freedom and rebirth. And, of course, the American Adam is now a perfectly integrated hero. But there is little to mediate.

The opening shot establishes the pastoral elements of archetypal America: from the bank of a river through trees in the soft, dappled afternoon light a huge paddleboat lazily makes its way upriver; over this shot a banjo plays "Steamboat Round the Bend" and printed titles emerge on the screen telling us, "Time: The early 90's; Place: The

"Nostalgia at its best": Eden, in Steamboat Round the Bend. *Courtesy of* Phototeque.

Mississippi River." This shot conveys the serenity, beauty, and unity Americans hungered for in their New Eden. While the remaining shots carry us in classical Hollywood editing style from the general to the specific, Ford endows them with a lyricism that might not have been present with another director. The film is filled with this kind of imagery: Fleety Belle (Anne Shirley) transfixed in sorrow against the moonlit river; Fleety Belle and Dr. John (Will Rogers) searching the river together for the New Moses (Berton Churchill); the two riverboat captains joshing competitively from their cabins; and Duke's (John McGuire) view from his jail cell of the *Claremont Queen* rounding the bend just in time to save him from the gallows. But the central image is, of course, an American celebration—the start of a riverboat race. Four huge riverboats line up and the riverbank is teeming with people. This is nostalgia at its best. The formal unity of the composition, the perfect sense of framing, and the slightly high-angle long shot all give this shot the look of a historical tableau. Yet there is still a freedom of movement, an impression of life bursting the confines of the frame, and a sense of spontaneity. One senses the power of American commerce, the edge of American competitiveness, the beauty of American nature, and the energy of American people. With Will Rogers at the wheel using every bit of his native ingenuity America can win the race

and save the day. This might well have been the central message that
this film made deep in America's bleak Depression. For, as Leo Marx
noted in *The Machine in the Garden*, "The pastoral ideal has been used
to define the meaning of America ever since the age of discovery."[4]

The world of *Steamboat* is innocent in the extreme, comically and
truly so. For instance, when Dr. John turns Duke, the suspected murderer, over to the sheriff (wonderfully rendered by Eugene Pallette),
the sheriff throws the keys down and tells Duke to "Just open her up
and make yourself at home. Take the first bed you take a likin' to. And,
Doc just hang the keys on the front doorknob, will you? I'll be seein'
you in the morning about breakfast time. Goodnight." In this Eden
Will Rogers has few conflicts to resolve. There is no real violence; no
murder has actually taken place. Only Fleety Belle's swamp people
make trouble, which Dr. John resolves when he absent-mindedly discovers that the knife he has in his hand has argument-winning potential. The plot of the film, finding the New Moses so that Duke can be
set free to marry Fleety Belle, is just a flimsy excuse to give Dr. John
something to do in Eden. The tension is manufactured. So the New
Adam in *Steamboat* lacks the problem-solving wisdom, the deeply
etched lines of loneliness, and the residue of memory and loss that are
so much a part of Judge Priest and Dr. Bull. Instead, Dr. John frolics
up and down the river, indulges in repartee, and digresses at will.

The centerpiece of the film is the steamboat race. In Eden compe-
tition is not an end in itself, so Dr. John enters because that is the only
way he can get down the river to find the New Moses. But once entered, he bets his entire boat, even though it is thoroughly out-
matched, and tries to win by any device (anticipating young Abe
Lincoln's tug-o-war trickery when he hitches the rope to a wagon).
When Dr. John finally wins, he exhibits absolutely no interest in the
trophy. Instead, he races off to save Duke.

For the American Adam, history is expendable. Dr. John owned a
floating wax museum that he used as a money-making attraction. When
he purchased the museum it was filled with European kings and
queens, but he immediately transforms them in a wonderfully comic
scene into southern heroes—including the fictional characters, Little
Eva and Uncle Tom. When, in the final rush toward the finish line,
the *Claremont Queen* needs more fuel, into the flames go the American wax figures. It is more important to save Duke and win the race
than to preserve the paraffin past. This exemplifies the pragmatic humanism of the American Adam.

With America's past and "demon rum" fueling the flames, the *Claremont Queen* places first, Duke is set free, and Dr. John wins a superlative riverboat. True love now steers Dr. John's new riverboat as he
lounges serenely on deck. This is the end of a film that leaves no lin-

gering doubts as to unresolved conflicts or discordant ambiguity. This is the American Eden and Dr. John is the American Adam. Perhaps Ford and Rogers felt they were helping turn Americans away from the doldrums of Depression by showing possibilities of Eden. Will Rogers died in an airplane accident shortly after the film was completed. Ford never made such an unmitigated Edenic film again.

2

The Myth of the American Frontier: *Stagecoach,* *Young Mr. Lincoln,* and *Drums along the Mohawk*

THE YEAR 1939 was spectacularly prolific for both American cinema and John Ford. It is the year in which he made his mark with three films that may appear quite different: *Stagecoach* catapulted the traditional Western into the sound era and was another personal triumph for Ford who again (as with *The Informer*) went outside his contract studio to find a producer for what was to become, again, a critical and financial success; *Young Mr. Lincoln* was a Darryl Zanuck project that humanized a legend; and *Drums along the Mohawk* was another Zanuck production meant to evoke in ravishing color the community spirit of an outpost during America's revolutionary beginnings.

Different though they may be, they form, with no intent on Ford's part, a kind of frontier trilogy. Both before and after 1939 Ford's films always concerned frontiers: frontier settings, frontier eras, and frontier characters. What made 1939 different is that the myth and the reality of the frontier became the actual subjects of the films. Certainly Ford's early reputation as a director with affinities for the western and frontier settings meant that producers would think of him when those kinds of scripts became available. But in 1939 it seems as though Zanuck, Ford, and their screenwriters had absorbed the significance of America's frontier identity. By this time Frederick Jackson Turner's "frontier hypothesis" was well known. Ford's 1939 work could be taken as the filmic embodiment of Turner's thesis that "the existence of an area of free land, its continuous recession, and the advance of American settlement westward explain American development."[1] Turner's "successive Wests" can be found in *Drums along the Mohawk's* eastern deep forest, *Young Mr. Lincoln's* midwestern frontier, and *Stagecoach's* old southwest. Turner was a historian who demonstrated the reality of this development; Ford was a romancer who needed to fuse that reality to the frontier's myth. The myth of America's frontiers had been growing during the nineteenth century and by 1939 was substantially in place. Turner's thesis grounded that myth in historical data endowing the frontier with unmatched significance. And Ford, too, though he had a

The American frontier: the stage entering the wilderness in Stagecoach.

romantic attachment to the frontier, always took great care to anchor his films' mythic narratives to realistic mise-en-scènes. So his three 1939 films, for instance, stand as filmic benchmarks for each particular frontier setting. In fact, it was the Western that set the standard for the realistic mise-en-scène in American films, though it is rarely given credit for it. Too often the realistic subject matter of American neo-realism has been taken to be the beginning of American film realism.

The myth of the American frontier was the mortar that held together the various elements of Ford's vision. It was the frontier that fired Ford's imagination, as it had so many artists before him. In that vast space between civilization and the wilderness, or, in historian Walter Prescott Webb's dichotomy, between the metropolis and the frontier, lay the adventure, distance, and exotica of romance.[2] Romances were born out of frontiers where the knights could continue the civilizing mission of the founding kings, without wholly acquiescing to the limitations of civilization. The knight, grounded in reality, could take flight into the unknown and uncharted regions of the world, the imagination, and the psyche. He represented the dreams that men and women hoped and half-believed could come true. The knight was a mediator grounded in both the real and the marvelous and serene in his ability to resolve the cultural, human, and psychological tensions posed by civilization and the wilderness.

Walter Prescott Webb believed that, "the Great Frontier will take its place as a factor of the first magnitude in modern history," ranking alongside "the Renaissance, the Reformation, the American and French Revolutions, the Industrial Revolution."[3] America became the last great hope of the disenchanted and disenfranchised. It was the frontier of the mind, the spirit, and the world, the final mythic realm of the modern world. It was the New Eden, the New Arcadia, the New Canaan, and, of course, the New World. More prosaically, it was also New England. It held out the modern world's hope of rebirth. Out of the wilderness would emerge a new civilization. All the ingredients of the imagination were already in place: a verdant land, an aboriginal race, a decadent European origin, and a zealous breed of adventurers.

But it was not the New England experiment that captured America's imagination. The frontier needed to move out beyond the confines of Puritan theocracy. So it began again—out West. Here the New Adam could be reborn as the American Adam, here individualism could flourish, and here democracy could be born. And in that wisp of time, one century essentially, the "Great Frontier" opened and closed. By 1893 Frederick Jackson Turner proclaimed the frontier thesis of American history, and almost immediately the frontier closed. The settling of the American West, compressed into such a short period of time and so rich in its polarities of wilderness and civilization, became a perfect model for the development of civilization. The Western film collapsed the West into an even narrower time frame, from the end of the Civil War to the end of the century. In this way one or two generations could span an entire civilization and one hero could find himself straddling as many as three stages of civilization. This mythic world's temporal unity transformed it into a microcosm, while its spatial breadth gave it the sweep of a macrocosm. The myth of the frontier became *the* myth of American culture because it embodied the essential ingredients of the American dream: land, open spaces, change, equality, individual freedom, rebirth, and economic opportunity.

By 1939 the fact of the frontier was virtually dead. The gangster films of the 1930s spoke to this reality. The frontier had been turned inside out; the frontiersmen who had been able to escape society through "successive Wests" were now forced to become urban sociopaths. The final manifestation of the Western hero (pre-science fiction) was the urban detective. Ford seemed unsuited to working with this vision of urban decay, as *The Whole Town's Talking* can testify. In 1939 Ford still held out hope for those qualities that the frontier embodied: the American Adam (John Wayne and Henry Fonda were youthful extensions of Will Rogers), the progress of an American frontier civilization (*Stagecoach* and *Drums Along the Mohawk*), and the American democrat (*Young Mr. Lincoln*). But since the reality of an actual frontier no longer existed, Ford, philosophically speaking, had to develop these still-viable frontier qualities within the framework of myth. Thus, he was drawn to historical subjects set in pivotal eras that could be or already were cloaked in the aura of legend. Ford was no naive romancer. As a voracious reader of history, he knew the facts. But he was also a storyteller, a filmmaker, and, by temperament, a romantic. He was perfectly suited, then, to make romances.

The very nature of American filmmaking, apart from Ford, was drawn to the romance. As a visual and aural form, film is grounded in physical reality, and American cinema's popular narrative tradition demanded certain realistic premises. Yet, at the same time, these narratives rely on larger-than-life heroes and heroines who are usually the questers of romance searching for their true identities (and hence America's) which must be based on moral precepts. The stories are broad and sweeping with large doses of adventurous action. Finally, the majority of these films have either conscious or unconscious mythic structures. As a medium of militantly popular culture—one which *must* hook a broad segment of the American public and hook them powerfully—mythic archetypes are the most effective lure. The broadest, most common, and hence richest rubric is the American dream. The question is not how many American films do address some aspect of the American dream, but how few do not. The frontier myth of the American dream provided for American culture. The American dream alone posits attitudes without continuity, whereas the frontier, poised as it is between the wilderness and civilization, implies movement through both time and space with values attached to each epoch. If, as Turner noted, the frontier explains "American *development*," then the myth of the frontier might be able to heighten and compress that reality to the point that through its truth and imaginative power it becomes America's one, overriding foundation tale. Certainly film has contributed more than its share to this foundation myth. The Western romance is the form that the foundation myth took, which in John Ford's case I have identified as the myth of American civilization.

Ford's traditional Westerns (those that are concerned with neither the cavalry nor social issues) take the myth of American civilization as their subject, which means that they are about America's search for the ideal civilization based on the most positive elements of the American dream. This journey takes Americans out of and back into the wilderness, onto the frontier and past it, into civilization and back out of it. The search takes them from the post-Civil War era toward and sometimes into the twentieth century and out into "successive Wests." The goal is a free, just, and humane civilization; however, this goal is found neither in the polarized civilization nor in the savage wilderness, but in that middle state of balance and equilibrium, the frontier.

In 1939 Ford's films expressed the possibility of a young and vital American civilization, tempered only by the hardships of the past and the tragedies of the future. This America was personified in the innocently rough-hewn Ringo Kid (John Wayne) and the compassionate and hopeful prostitute, Dallas (Claire Trevor), in *Stagecoach;* the young, gangly, and human Abe Lincoln (Henry Fonda) whose loss of Ann Rutledge (Pauline Moore) motivates him and foreshadows his tragedies; and the sturdy yeoman, Gil Martin (Henry Fonda), and his more civilized wife, Lana (Claudette Colbert), who together forge a home and family on the Mohawk Valley frontier.

During and after World War II Ford experienced America's growth in technology, wealth, materialism, institutional bureacracy, and legalism. The film business was no longer a freewheeling pioneer industry; America's open land was being trammeled by urban sprawl and scientific cultivation; and our government had become a world power. Civilization had overtaken the frontier. One could argue that there were other eras in American history when this occurred just as dramatically, but this was the turning point that Ford experienced. His response to this melancholy truth was to make films that more pungently questioned the faith that the myth of American civilization had placed in progress. As Ford aged, the frontier reached the point of diminishing returns, so that in *The Man Who Shot Liberty Valance*, for instance, he could stretch the frontier no longer—it had become civilized. This was rationalized by calling it a "garden." The Western mythos allowed Ford to continue making films in that frontier space known as the West, but the mid-twentieth-century realities of restriction forced him to counter with heroes who were older and more complex, ambivalent, and reclusive. The spatial frontiers may have been closed, but the psychological ones hadn't. This fact kept Ford's films modern, while his enduring faith in the infinite resourcefulness and humanity of common people kept him from becoming an embittered anachronism. The frontier may have literally disappeared, but the aging heroes of Ford's films whom time had passed by survive in their timeless, mythic world. They in turn pass on their moral strength and vision to their younger progeny who have been selected to carry on and fight for the values of the frontier. Ford's films are meant to serve the same function as his aging heroes. Ford in his most private thoughts might actually have seen himself through his filmmaking as a conveyor of the flame. Myths are, after all, moral lessons.

At any rate, in 1939 all three of Ford's films were concerned with frontiers, and all three have significant fences that ground the metaphoric line of demarcation between civilization and the wilderness in a physical reality. In the beginning of *Stagecoach* the travelers pass a wooden rail fence that materializes in both the middle of the desert and on the outskirts of Tonto, that "civilized" frontier town. The stage enters a landscape that could in no way be described as anything other than wilderness. This is cinema's first glimpse of the primordial formations in Monument Valley (this same shot will be virtually repeated in *My Darling Clementine*, another civilization film). In *Young Mr. Lincoln* another wooden rail fence appears as Ann and Abe walk along the river. But it is not until an opening occurs in the fence that they are able to express their love for each other. This fence, erected on the frontier by the forces of civilization, prevents them from a true oneness, both with each other and with nature. And finally, in *Drums Along the Mohawk*, after Gil's and Lana's extremely civilized wedding, her parents watch as their covered wagon passes the large stone wall that marks the boundary of their substantial Albany estate. This shot and this wall express the same metaphoric meaning in the same way as the stagecoach passing the fence in Ford's earlier film. Fences and walls are what human beings build to signify that they have created a civilized place. Ford's frontier heroes must pass beyond those barriers if they are to find themselves, be at one with nature, and found a new civilization. These may be barriers between civilization and the wilderness, but they also help define the frontier. The frontier always begins on the wilderness side of the fence and ends where those nonindigenous people with civilizing inclinations no longer settle. As these pioneers march out into the wilderness, it recedes at the same rate that civilization encroaches upon it. The frontier in the myth of the American frontier is that ephemeral state that embodies the American dream. Some of the great film pioneers made Westerns before Ford got his chance: E. S. Porter, Thomas Ince, D. W. Griffith, Cecil B. DeMille, and Allan Dwan. Yet, by 1917 in Ford's first Western feature, *Straight Shooting*, he had not only absorbed the basic structures of this still-primitive genre, but had enhanced them. Ford's career really began when he teamed up with Harry Carey who played the offbeat Western star, Cheyenne Harry. Between 1917 and 1921 they made twenty-four films together. They were true collaborators, often sitting around making up the stories between them. When their relationship ended, they were both established figures in the movie industry, but their salaries reflected the importance of the star ($2,250 a week) over the director ($300 a week).

Ford's concern for visual style can be traced back to their first feature together, *Straight Shooting* (1917), which is also Ford's earliest extant film. In it there are a number of his favorite visual motifs: the framing devices of doorways, windows, and canyons shot from the inner darkness out into depth of field light; the alternating high- and low-angle establishing shots of grazing cows on the range suggestive of the opening shots of *My Darling Clementine*. Authentic detail and dramatic settings coexist in Ford's use of rainstorms, horizons, and pastoral glens. Also included in this film are the spectacular stunts, frisky horses, and eccentric moments added for spontaneity. For instance, an actor fell off his horse and into the river during shooting; Ford kept this shot in the film. Throughout his career Ford continued to retain these kinds of unexpected mistakes. There are also instances of his willingness to indulge in comic digressions. After the climactic gunfight, for example, a cowboy steals some jam from the heroine's cupboard. It is a wonderful yet narratively unnecessary touch.

Perhaps the most compelling aspect of this early film is Ford's mature approach to characterization. In his interview with Peter Bogdanovich, Ford said that his early films with Harry Carey "weren't shot-'em-ups, they were character stories." At a time when theater and movies fed the public knights in shining armor and black-hatted villains, Ford and Carey not only gave Cheyenne Harry a complex persona, but did so through his relationship with other characters. They endowed him with enough human foibles to make him acceptable to more discerning audiences. Cheyenne Harry was a wanted man with a thousand dollars on his head, which we discover in one of the most bizarre entrances a cowboy hero has ever made: Harry suddenly leans out from a branch like a wood sprite with a Cheshire grin and wild eyes, as he acknowledges himself as the wanted man. Harry is always caught in the middle, torn by conflicting feelings. This, of course, was crucial to Ford's enduring conception of a hero's character development. Finally, the shoot-out between Harry and Fremont begins in the same style as the great classical Westerns. The dominant camera placement is behind and to the right of the hero. As the tension builds, there are intercuts between the men's faces. But Ford confounds the viewer by having the two men walk right past each other. The shoot-out becomes a game of cat and mouse around a small shack played out with rifles (a Ford favorite) rather than the standard six-shooters. Ford always tried to surprise us with this most ritualized Western event. Even the heroine becomes involved. Instead of being the coy, helpless type, she leaps on a horse and furiously rides for help. She is also portrayed as a human, stabilizing force for both Harry and the West. *Straight Shooting* is an extraordinary film, a gold mine of Fordiana.

In 1921 Ford jumped at the chance to work at the larger and better-financed Fox Studio. He worked under an exclusive contract for the next ten years at Fox, where he made his transition to sound and solidified his reputation. This was an important step because Fox provided a support system of money and talent that allowed him to become more versatile, to direct pictures with a larger budget, and to understand the uses of power in a large studio. At Universal he had begun to learn the craft of filmmaking; at Fox he began to learn the art. He worked with two of his most important cameramen, George Schneiderman (*The Iron Horse*, *Three Bad Men*, and the Will Rogers trilogy) and Joseph August (*Men without Women*, *The Informer*, *Mary of Scotland*, and *They Were Expendable*). His long relationship with screenwriter Dudley Nichols began at Fox.

At Fox Ford began to experiment with the four styles that would mark his work through 1948: (1) the studio assignments that Ford tried to infuse with touches of this own (*Cameo Kirby*, *Kentucky Pride*, *Riley the Cop*, and *Up the River*); (2) the Expressionistic dramas (*Four Sons* and *Hangman's House*); (3) the relaxed, anecdotal pieces of Americana (*Just Pals* and *Lightnin'*); (4) the allegorical epic Westerns (*The Iron Horse* and *Three Bad Men*). During the late 1930s and 1940s he varied and reduced these styles. But not until 1948, after *Three Godfathers*, was he able finally to unify these styles in his great Westerns that were both powerfully epic and anecdotally relaxed.

Dwan's 1916 Western *The Good Bad Man* most likely introduced the explicit ambiguity of character that Ford and the Western were later to exploit fully. In 1923 James Cruze directed the first large-scale historical Western, *The Covered Wagon*, which Ford bettered a year later with *The Iron Horse*. In *The Iron Horse* (1924) Ford was re-creating history and telling a love story—his favorite format. There is no question that this film has a place in film history, but it does not equal *Three Bad Men* Ford's greatest silent film. There are times in *The Iron Horse* when the narrative action wavers out of control. Melodrama and static dialogue undermine the visual authenticity and edited rhythm. The fusion of personal stories and historical events is generally forced and gimmick-ridden. Finally, the film's single-minded view that technological progress is good, despite the sacrifices, lacks the compelling ambivalence that contributes to the greatness of Ford's later Westerns.

Still, this film has so many Fordian touches that it remains one of his primers: the establishing shot of pastoral sheep and children in an age of innocence; the mystical and romantic urge to follow one's destiny; the shadows of the attacking Indians on the train; the importance of immigrants and the working man's point of view. Even folk songs are in this silent film. The grave diggers' life-force matter-of-factness juxtaposed with the grieving wife is life-and-death Fordiana; the touch of a loyal dog humanizes an Indian's death; there is a heroine who has the courage to stand and fight when the male workers won't; the "three musketeers" device of Ford's silent and early sound pictures expresses comic relief and loyal comradeship.

But one scene in particular shows Ford's new confidence in his manipulation of film. The film's climax is the long-awaited showdown between the hero, Davy (George O'Brien), and Bauman, the evil Indian/white man who murdered his father. It occurs during an Indian attack. Bauman had killed Davy's father with an axe; so, in line with Ford's love of visual and thematic symmetry, Davy attacks Bauman with an axe. As they struggle, both are framed by two wagons; in the background the attacking Indians race past in their circle raid. Then, just as Davy is choking Bauman to death, Ford intercuts a series of extremely powerful shots of Pawnee Indians coming to the rescue of the beleaguered railroad workers. They come at a right-to-left diagonal, breaking the static foreground struggle of Davy and Bauman and the horizontal movement of the attacking Indians. The Pawnees ride toward and past the camera, first in a long shot, and then a medium shot. In a remarkable close-up they flash by the camera. The final cut returns us back to the dead villain. This set of shots has a tremendous visceral effect: the crosscutting, the foreground-background tension, the increased rhythm of both edited and mise-en-scène movement, and finally the stillness of death and accomplished vengeance. No climax this visually powerful appears in Ford's earlier extant films.

These films combined the three major strains of the early Westerns: the dime-novel melodrama; sweeping, violent action; and historical slices of the American West.

But it was Ford's brilliant synthesis in *Three Bad Men* (1926) that brought to fruition the conventions, codes, themes, and stylistic characteristics of the silent Western. Ford seemed to have learned from his mistakes in *The Iron Horse*. This time he reversed the importance of the historical to the personal, making the land rush and the opening of the West no more than an integral backdrop to the personal stories. The tale itself is more intriguing. The unvarnished hero plays second fiddle to the "three bad men," who are beguiling in their roles as shady but loyal protectors of a tough, saucy girl stranded on her way to the land rush. In *Three Bad Men* Ford has a greater understanding of visual composition and a stronger sense of the film's rhythmic design. One shot in particular foreshadows the way Ford was able to control the mise-en-scène in a long take. Two of the "bad" men who are trying to find a husband for the heroine follow a dapper runt into a dance hall. The camera is set up to capture the action in one shot: the runt dances with a girl, while Mike (J. Farrell McDonald) performs a pantomime of their dance alongside (camera dollies forward with them slightly); the runt rushes away from the girl and the two "bad" men pull their guns to shoot him, when, at that very moment, a short, fat, traveling newspaper editor with a hilarious gait walks right through them with such determined and expressionless aplomb that the two "bad" men follow him in amazed curiosity. As he walks toward the camera, it dollies back to its original position, and, just as it gets there, with perfect timing, a portable bar is rolled on-screen in front of the editor. He nonchalantly orders a drink, as though the bar had been there forever.

By the end of the silent era Ford had made more Westerns than any other director. His reputation was based on that genre, not that it did him any good. During the early sound days at Fox Ford was tied to the soundstage, so other directors at other studios tried to keep the Western alive: King Vidor, Henry Hathaway, and DeMille at Paramount, and Raoul Walsh at Warner Brothers.

During the 1930s the Western was put on hold, with the exception of cheap "B" versions. In 1937 Ford bought the rights to Ernest Haycox's short story "Stage to Lordsburg," and with Dudley Nichols wrote the script for *Stagecoach*. But no studio was interested, believing that Westerns had become a decidedly stale commodity for sound-era audiences. Only Walter Wagner, an independent producer with a one-picture commitment to United Artists, was interested. United Artists agreed to finance it only if the budget was kept to an unusually low $392,000. The rest is, shall we say, Western history. *Stagecoach* became, at least in the judgment of the influential French film scholar, André Bazin, "the ideal example of the maturity of a style brought to classic perfection."[4] While Bazin saw it as the fully realized end result of a genre's development, more recent critics are inclined to view it instead as the beginning of a renaissance in America's most richly significant film genre. Though Ford did not invent the Western, he certainly deepened its resonances and contributed to its body. With *Stagecoach* he reinvented the Western for cinema's transition era. *Stagecoach* firmly established the Western's myth (the American frontier), mythic polarity (civilization versus wilderness), and form (romance). Finally, after World War II, in 1946, Ford directed *My Darling Clementine*, the film that launched the Western's third era, its Golden Age, which lasted until, roughly, 1969. This era produced a vast body of beautiful, powerful, and significant films. During this period all facets of the Western mythos were examined. Ford's own career mirrored the Western's development: he was learning his craft, while the Western was establishing itself as a genre; both he and the Western entered maturity together in 1939; and, finally, the Western's darkening complexity and psychological probing were reflected in Ford's own late period. By 1973 both Ford and the Western were dead.

A few scholars have categorized the narrative patterns of Westerns. The most useful are Will Wright's four-plot structures (Classical Plot, Transition Theme, Vengeance Variation, and Professional Plot)[5] and Frank Gruber's seven-story types (the Union Pacific Story, the Ranch Story, the Empire Story, the Revenge Story, Custer's Last Stand, or the Cavalry and Indian Story, the Outlaw Story, and the Marshal Story).[6] Wright's scheme, though well worked out, exhibits, as he agrees, embarrassing flaws; for instance, no rubric exists for *Fort Apache*, *She Wore a Yellow Ribbon*, *Rio Grande*, *Wagon Master*, *Three Godfathers*, *The Horse Soldiers*, *Sergeant Rutledge*, *Two Rode Together*, and *Cheyenne Autumn*. Ford's shall we say, mainstream Westerns (*Stagecoach*, *My Darling Clementine*, *The Searchers*, and *The Man Who Shot Liberty Valance*), all fit Wright's Vengeance Variation. In Gruber's construct Ford's Westerns generally fall into the revenge, Custer's last stand, cavalry, and Indian categories. Thus, vengeance, military, and Indian subjects were Ford's primary traditionally Western interests.

However, many of his Westerns can also be realigned with his non-Westerns into categories that reflect his larger thematic concerns. For instance, his cavalry films and *The Horse Soldiers* could be classified with those pictures in which individualism is tested vis-à-vis the restrictive communities of the modern military: *They Were Expendable*, *The Long Gray Line*, and *The Wings of Eagles*. *Three Bad Men* and *Three Godfathers* have strong ties to Ford's biblical allegories, *The Informer* and *The Fugitive*. *Sergeant Rutledge*, *Two Rode Together*, and *Cheyenne Autumn* share an affinity with *Donovan's Reef* and *7 Women* as social-problem atonement films. The "pure" Westerns all have civilization as their subject: *The Searchers* explores its opposite, savagery, through the extremes of vengeance, while *The Iron Horse*, *Stagecoach*, *My Darling Clementine*, *Wagon Master*, and *The Man*

Who Shot Liberty Valance consider the effects of "successive Wests" as the frontier moves ever closer to civilization. In this myth of American civilization the Civil War and the subsequent forty years represent the pivotal era of American history, for it signaled a rebirth structured on division and unification. The post-Civil War West became the most potent frontier because from a twentieth-century perspective one could see the confrontation between a true wilderness and *modern* civilization. In this respect, both the time and the place made for a truly unique frontier. Out of this frontier there emerged frontiersmen who successfully mediated or unsuccessfully attempted to mediate the extremes of civilization and wilderness, man and nature, East and West, individual and community. The heroes of these romances were the cowboys, outlaws, cavalrymen, gamblers, stage drivers, adventurers, lawmen, Indians, farmers, wives, and prostitutes of the frontier who transcended the trivialities of safe, secure lives by forging precarious existences beyond the reaches of respectable, civilized societies.

The western frontier was the vessel into which the American dream could be poured, mixed, and separated: egalitarian yet individualistic, pragmatic yet idealistic, vast yet restrictive, just yet intolerant, agrarian yet mercantile, friendly yet dangerous, self-reliant yet cooperative. If the evolution of the western frontier stood as a microcosmic model for the development of American civilization, and since America has been conceived as the New World, then the story of the West could be read as the story of world civilization. From the perspective of America's first frontier stage, Europe was the decadent civilization, but in the post–Civil War West the American East took Europe's place. Only in the West could all people be free, live as equals, own land, move at will, make a fresh start, draw strength and moral purity from unspoiled nature. Southerners could regain their dignity, blacks could coexist, and immigrants could fit in. But since the frontier also tested these precepts, man's physical, psychological, moral, and ethical limits were stretched to the breaking point. As the frontier myth has it, the whole of human history can be played out in this mythically compressed and highly charged era.

In those few post-Civil War decades America could be seen to be swiftly transformed from a wilderness into a civilization. This is the myth, and, like all myths, the truth lies somewhere between the facts and the deeper structures of the accepted narratives. In 1939 Ford made three films about three different stages in America's frontier heritage, but it became quite clear that only the Western era could truly express the deep-seated concerns inherent in America's rush toward civilization. *Stagecoach* is Ford's first mature effort to address the problems of America's civilizing process. The films that most fully confront the issues of what civilization is, what is its worth, and what it means to be civilized are *Stagecoach*, *My Darling Clementine*, *The Searchers*, and *The Man Who Shot Liberty Valance*. It is, perhaps, not too surprising that these films expressed Ford's profound ambivalence about civilization's inexorable march out of the wilderness and past the frontier. But the pendulum of that ambivalence swung just as inexorably toward an ever-deepening skepticism of civilization's progress. Ford began as a vigorous advocate and ended as a melancholy doubter. The myth of civilization states that, as humankind tests itself in the wilderness and sheds it savagery, it progresses to the frontier where the forces of the wilderness and civilization are held in tension and equilibrium. There, communities are formed and laws are enacted that are intended to lead humankind toward an advanced state of social, cultural, governmental, and scientific existence. Though the American dream enunciates the positive qualities of this progression, Ford's films refuse to endorse the values of progress so wholeheartedly. Instead, there is an apex, the frontier, after which progress is shown to be both illusory and possible, and what is lost has more emotional resonance than what is gained.

Three of Ford's civilization films, *Stagecoach*, *Clementine*, and *Liberty Valance*, have a coherence in that they develop in succeeding order the progressive stages of the myth of American civilization; (1) the wilderness; (2) the frontier town; (3) the civilizing factors; (4) the possibility of the garden. For instance, *Stagecoach* is primarily grounded in the travelers' ordeal in the wilderness. *Clementine* is about the transition of the frontier town from being dominated by the wilderness to being dominated by civilizing factors. Finally, *Liberty Valance* chronicles the ascendancy of the civilizing factors and the possibility of the garden. *Stagecoach* accepts the primal powers of the wilderness; *Clementine* celebrates the equilibrium of the frontier; *Liberty Valance* mourns the loss of the frontier, while it proffers a grudging respect for the civilizing factors.

Vengeance and civilization stand in opposition to each other in these films. The code of civilization demands that retribution be rejected, yet that justice be done. The justice of the frontier is primarily that of the Old Testament, natural law, and medieval romances—in other words, the justice of the wilderness. But those who represent civilization abhor the violence of this code, preferring the court of law. So the frontier is caught between these two forces. The civilizing factors in these films are often shown to be impotent in the face of wilderness violence and confused as to how to administer justice. This necessitates the emergence of the hero-mediator, a figure of mythic proportions who had been wronged and seeks vengeance. However, he has been humanized during his search, to the extent that he can continue his vengeance quest without falling into the abyss of savagery. Only these frontier mediators who have their roots in the wilderness and who have been humanized but not civilized are physically, morally, and ethically equipped to carry out the ritual acts of retribution. Only after they accept their humanizing by the civilizing factors can vengeance be called justice.

Stagecoach: American Civilization

The ending of *Stagecoach* gives us a glimpse into Ford's early ambivalence toward civilization. As Doc Boone (Thomas Mitchell) sends Ringo (John Wayne) and Dallas (Claire Trevor) off to begin another, presumably better, civilization across the border, he says sardonically, "Well, they're saved from the blessings of civilization." In 1939 Ford placed his faith in youth and new beginnings. The existing examples of civilization, the frontier towns of Tonto and Lordsburg, are pest holes of bigotry and debauchery. Ringo's ranch offers the possibility of a new civilization growing out of a garden, now that he has Dallas—his Eve—with her proven maternal instincts: "it's a nice place—a real nice place—trees—grass—water—there's a cabin half built. A man could live there—and a woman." So Doc, the cynically ironic sage, and Curly (George Bancroft), the paternalistic, pragmatic Marshal, are left to face "the blessings of civilization" alone. The wilderness has its virtues, however, for it is only through a confrontation with the hard emptiness and dangerous savagery of Monument Valley that the "civilized" passengers discover their moral sense. The passage through the wilderness teaches them to be truly civilized, not simply cultured. In *Stagecoach* the iconography is clearly enunciated as a rite of passage through no-man's-land: a fence running horizontally clearly marks the line between civilization and the wilderness; the road disappearing into the distance signifies the passengers' unknown future; the monument speaks to the primordial mysteries and overwhelming majesty of this vast and precarious wilderness. This shot introduces the dialectical relationships between civilization, wilderness, and savagery. In *Stagecoach* it indicates civilization's savagery and the wilderness's power to heal. A few shots later these people will pass beyond the pale through a cloud of dust, into a realm where they will be tested. For only in the wilderness can truly humanized individualism and community be measured.

Stagecoach is Ford's celebration of the wilderness's powers of regeneration. The two frontier towns are examples of degenerate civilization. The first, Tonto, is afflicted with "a foul disease called social prejudice," as Doc Boone aptly puts it when he is run out of town. The second, Lordsburg, is a hard, violent town. Both are wayward developments of civilization, though Ford depicts Tonto's upwardly mobile citizenry with a sharper eye and greater glee. For instance, when Dallas is being run out of town for prostitution, she gets on the stage even though Geronimo is on the warpath, saying, "there are worse things than Apaches." Ford immediately cuts to a reaction shot of the sour, hatchet-faced "ladies" of the Law and Order League. In this perfectly timed juxtaposition of language and image Ford has placed the Indians of the wilderness against the inhabitants of civilization, and found civilization wanting. The cure is a mythic return to the wilderness for a new rite of passage and a rebirth of American civilization. This is the mythic function of the stagecoach's journey.

Each traveler, then, is a mythic character from America's folk heritage, their characterizations always teetering between clichéd stereotypes and resonant archetypes. They achieve archetypal dimensions in *Stagecoach* by having been acurately cast, by acting out their roles to perfection, and by infusing complexity into simplistically outlined characterizations. Doc Boone, as the alcoholic, jaded, generous philosopher-outcast, is an excellent example of a folk type who constantly reappears in Ford's mythic world. Doc's ability to see through the shams of the civilized world has forced it to exile him. He stays drunk so as to blur his vision and protect his soul from the ravages of civilization. During his exile he is called upon to deliver a child. The possibility of performing the elementary rite of bringing life into the wilderness drives the drunken stupor out of him. Suddenly he becomes paterfamilias, giving sober advice to Dallas and stopping Luke Plummer from taking the shotgun out of the bar. Once he has sent Dallas and Ringo off to begin a new and presumably better civilization (because it will be a true frontier) he can return to his role as society's drunken and disreputable philosopher.

Peacock (Donald Meek, whose last name personified his role) is the stock weakling who lacks courage and forthrightness, a traveling salesman who belongs in the bosom of his "dear family," a deliciously comic figure who seems more reverend than whiskey drummer. Peacock is discovered standing alone at the end of an empty bar, a tiny, incongrous figure who calls the bartender "brother." But when he turns out to be a whiskey drummer, Doc, discovering his profession, immediately takes him under his wing. Our first images of Peacock are confounding. What is a man who looks like a reverend doing in a bar? But then, what is a man who looks and acts as he does doing as a whiskey drummer? Peacock will be tested through his encounters with the other passengers, the birth of the child, and the Indian attack. When Peacock casts a vote for staying until Mrs. Mallory is ready to travel, regardless of the danger, Doc, the moral arbiter, pronounces judgment on Peacock, "Spoken like a man, Reverend." Doc is able to see through

Peacock's societal image. Instead of a cowardly whiskey drummer, he sees a moral man.

Lucy Mallory (Louise Platt), the overcivilized social snob, is transformed by childbirth and Dallas's compassion. Hatfield (John Carradine), the doomed gambler and wayward Southern aristocrat, is the tragic transitional character caught between the wilderness and civilization. Like Doc Holliday in *My Darling Clementine*, Hatfield is the rootless easterner whose past he shrouds in mystery. Fleeing civilized society, his rebellion has led to a life of crime on the frontier. Driven beyond the frontier, this flawed precursor of the heroic mediator dies in the violence of the wilderness. In a final gesture of inbred gentility Hatfield redeems himself. He has been drawn instinctively to the Eastern lady, Mrs. Mallory. Together they epitomize the decadent values of civilization. Hatfield's death represents the death of the East and its corrupt influence on the West, while Mrs. Mallory lives and changes in order to bring new life onto the frontier.

Gatewood (Berton Churchill) is the self-satisfied, crooked banker, the presumed pillar of society who is also its most despicable representative. The stage's other "civilized" characters are redeemed, but not this pompous hypocrite. He is continually diminished and isolated in the mise-en-scène. He is introduced in a slightly high-angle shot, then separated from his surroundings by one-shot close-ups. Finally, he is completely missing from the screen during the growing cohesion of the travelers. His entire being is the antithesis of Ford's values: he was the banker-embezzler of the Depression era and his reactionary politics marked him as a man who cared nothing for the plight of the common people. But it is his pomposity that dooms him forever in Ford's eyes.

Curly (George Bancroft), the Marshal, is the beneficent patriarch of the wilderness, the representative of reasonable and flexible frontier authority (as a federal Marshal he is not responsible for Tonto's puritanical inquisition). During the frontier's evolution Curly has emerged from the ranks of the cowhands. Curly becomes the institutional instrument for democratic action. He understands that a tightrope stretches over the frontier holding both free democracy and authority in an uneasy balance. So, while he takes a vote at each way station, he continues to hold Ringo's vote in a proxy, tell Buck how to vote, and overlook Dallas. By the end of the film he participates in Ringo's escape. As with all of Ford's authority figures, Curly upholds the spirit, not the letter, of the law.

Buck (Andy Devine), the stage driver, is the wilderness's eternal fool. Nothing touches him. He exists in his own world, lost in his own thoughts (for comic effect), and concerned only with feeding himself and his huge Mexican family. Buck is endowed with cosmic stupidity, and, as with Shakespeare's fools, he seems at one with the natural order. For instance, it is Buck who invests the child's birth with the magical union of humanness and nature when he mistakes the infant's first cry for that of a coyote. The child has been touched by the wilderness. It is born there and is christened "Little Coyote" by this odd band of now-unified travelers.

The birth of Mrs. Mallory's baby is the central event of the film, for it humanizes all who attend it. It is the mythic event, concealed from the audience and passengers alike until the very moment of its occurrence. Bickering and conflict had characterized the journey, but with the greatest danger lying ahead the travelers need a catalyst to unite them. This event also cements the central relationship of the film, Ringo's and Dallas's mythic joining of man and woman, wilderness and civilization, present and future, individual and community. When Ringo watches Dallas hold Mrs. Mallory's baby (symbolically, the child belongs to the society—a kind of Christ child), he sees in Dallas a woman to love and the mother of a new civilization. This is a moment of community where Dallas and Ringo can emerge from their trials as the outcasts of a bankrupt society to forge a new world. The past doesn't count. Ringo tells her he knows all he wants to know about her. He knows her the way all of Ford's lovers know each other, by looking deeply into each other's eyes. These are always special moments in Ford pictures, executed with purity and electricity.

Ford took the cliché of the prostitute-with-the-heart-of-gold and cajoled Claire Trevor into giving the role dimension as the brassy frontier woman, the compassionate woman-mother, and vulnerable outcast. What Dallas and Ringo share is a belief in survival, that essential code of the frontier. She says to Ringo, "Well, you gotta live, no matter what happens." He agrees, "Yeah, that's it." This common faith triggers his proposal to her. In the wilderness Dallas can be seen for what she is; in the wilderness Dallas and Ringo realize what they have in common and what they can bring to each other.

The Ringo Kid was the quintessential hero of thirties' Westerns. His youth, size, power, innocence, vulnerability, and quiet sense of self marked him for greatness in this fresh, new world. But the hero must also be an outcast, an outlaw, a child of the wilderness, and a mediator. Ford's and Nichols's sense of the dramatic led them to introduce Ringo last, after the stage was filled and out of town. The stage must pass through three metaphorical boundaries before it can be truly in the wilderness: the fence, the cloud of dust, and the river.

Then, in one of Ford's most explicitly mythical shots, the Ringo Kid simply materializes on the landscape, saddle and blanket in one hand, Winchester in the other. Naked (i.e., horseless), yet dominating the

The mythical hero; two images in one shot: Ringo (John Wayne) dominating his environment (top); and as the vulnerable, questioning innocent (bottom).

powerful monuments behind him, he twirls his Winchester in a gesture so loaded with size and control that he is instantly recognized as *the* frontier hero. The camera faces him so directly, in a slightly low angle, that the rapid dollying-in transforms the shot into a powerfully subjective experience in which Ringo faces down the onrushing team of horses. In an act of supreme confidence he yells, "Hold it!" But the camera keeps moving in on him, until, finally, it rests on a huge close-up of a slightly puzzled, innocent, vulnerable Ringo. Yet the size of the image, the delicate low angle, the entire action of confronting the stage invests him with great power. The paradoxical imagery shows off Ford's powers as well. The Western now has its defining hero, the one against which all others must be measured.

When Ringo gets into the stage, he sits down on the floor between the passengers. He has taken the position of a mediator and will immediately begin to act as one. He is the only passenger inside the coach not tainted by civilization because he has been taken aboard out in the wilderness. So, from a physical, moral, and cultural position he mediates the conflicts between Hatfield (South, chivalrous) and Doc (North, natural hedonist), Hatfield and the two women, Hatfield and Gatewood. Each conflict is edited so as to emphasize Ringo's middle ground: crosscutting between antagonists with Ringo interceding after a few passes. Ringo's approach is to begin with authority ("Sit down, mister"), then switch to boyish apologies ("Doc don't mean no harm").

Ford and Nichols created a civilization whose inhabitants are placed on a moral continuum from positive to negative: from Dallas and Ringo to Doc and Curly to Peacock to Mrs. Mallory to Hatfield and, finally, to Gatewood. Buck stands outside this scale, by virtue of his comic amorality. The film's basic proposition is that those who have been driven out of civilization and who are able to adapt to the ways of the wilderness are the truly civilized characters, the positive forces of the frontier. Those who live and act naturally and without pretense are the folk heroes of the West: the innocent cowboy, the prostitute with the heart of gold, the friendly marshal, the comic stage driver, the dignified Indians. These are the individualists who can help transform the transitional figures. The continuum reveals that those at each extreme are the least affected by the journey's rite of passage, while those in the middle, Peacock and Mrs. Mallory, change dramatically. The further one progresses down the scale (i.e., toward the negative, more "civilized" end), the more one hides his or her essential self behind clothes and poses. Thus, layers of disembodying cultural veneer are added to human beings in the name of civilization.

Young as Ringo is, he has been tempered by the violence of both civilization and the wilderness. Violence is at the heart of every Western. It is the foundation of the myth of the frontier and has shaped the evolution of American civilization. Richard Slotkin in his important book, *Regeneration Through Violence: The Mythology of the American Frontier, 1600–1860*, presents a convincing thesis for the predominance of violence in American culture: "The first colonists saw in America an opportunity to regenerate their fortunes, their spirits and the power of their church and nation; but the means to that regeneration ultimately became the means of violence, and the myth of regeneration through violence became the structuring metaphor of the American experience."[7] The battle between the forces of civilization and the wilderness was a fight to the death. Violence paved the way for new settlements. The frontier towns, then, engendered more violence. The Western, interested in moral issues and quests, took the medieval romance as its model and chose vengeance as the form of violence most richly expressive of both personal and cultural conflict. The Western adheres to Slotkin's thesis that only through violence could Americans on the frontier find regeneration. But the Western also questioned the mode and extent of violence necessary for regeneration.

In vengeance films the civilizing factors offer life instead of death. "Little Coyote's" birth is the first life force and Dallas's mothering the second. But, as Ringo tells Dallas, "there's some things a man just can't run away from." Dallas sets him straight on that old Western chestnut, "How can you talk about your life and my life when you're throwing 'em away?" And, surprisingly, for the Western genre but not for Ford, she talks him into escaping rather than fighting. He is willing to reject vengeance and turn his back on the wilderness for the opportunity of beginning a new civilization. Of course, circumstances intervene. The hero must gain revenge. The point is, however, that in both rejecting vengeance and acting on it he maintains his role as a mediator. The Plummers must be killed so that Dallas and Ringo can begin a new stage of civilization, a new frontier. Ford's message is that regeneration must come through both an acceptance of the civilizing factors and the act of violence. Newly civilized yet outcasts, Ringo and Dallas ride into the sunset (West, toward the wilderness), to establish a new frontier, one less "civilized" and less violent than the old frontier.

Young Mr. Lincoln: The American Democrat

In the wilderness democracy could not survive because it was subject to Darwinian laws that protected neither the weak nor the minority. In civilization democracy becomes weakened by the legalisms and cowardice of institutionalization. Only on the frontier could democracy flourish. There the balance between freedom and restriction, self-interest and social responsibility, experience and knowledge, pragmatism and idealism, brutalization and refinement keeps democracy alive. Laws, rules, and codes are the fabric of civilization; their absence is the essence of the wilderness. When civilization institutionalized these laws and rules, they became ends unto themselves, thus removing them from the common people who created them. Democracy worked on the frontier because common folk developed laws and rules that pragmatically and flexibly gave order and safety to their still wilderness-imbued lives. On the frontier the spirit of the law took precedence over the letter of the law. However, the major threat to a democracy based on the spirit of the law is the unjust and inequitable interpretation and enforcement of the law by those who would use tyranny to take advantage of the leeway inherent in a law's spirit. This threat and its solution is the subject of *Young Mr. Lincoln*.

The solution lay primarily in the emergence from the frontier of a strong, mythic mediator committed to the principles of democracy—thus the myth of the American democrat. The elements of this myth that contribute to the solution of the threat to democracy are these: all conflicts must be resolved through mediation; individual, cultural, religious, and racial rights must be respected, and that respect reciprocated; a strong, decisive, humane, and pragmatic leader must rise from the common folk to mediate the conflicts inherent in a democracy; this leader should mediate through persuasion, humor, and tolerance; but if these methods fail, the democratic leader may persuade through either the threat of violence or violence itself; and finally the ideal solution should achieve freedom within consensus. To this end Will Rogers in *Steamboat Round the Bend* was the quintessential democrat. But that was Eden, whereas the world in 1939 bore little resemblance to that dream.

Young Mr. Lincoln is the film that most fully realizes the fusion of dream and reality. This is *the* film of the American democrat and young Abe Lincoln (Henry Fonda) is *the* American democrat. Every commentator agrees that *Young Mr. Lincoln* is a film of profound mythic dimensions. They also tend to assume that the myth is the myth of Lincoln. But could Lincoln have become such a mythic figure had he not embodied and symbolized a richer, deeper, and more culturally pervasive mythic complex—the myth of the American democrat on the American frontier, for instance?

Why is Lincoln the stuff of legends, not Washington or Jefferson? Washington and Jefferson have not become the true mythic figures of American culture because they did not embody and humanize in every way both the dream and the reality of American democracy and the American frontier. It was not enough to win America's independence and become the father of the country, or to draft the Declaration of Independence and become the architect of American democracy. Only

Lincoln was perfectly situated and equally prepared to take advantage of America's greatest watershed, the test of its democracy: through the accident of birth he sprang from humble frontier origins; through his force of personality and will he rose out of poverty and anonymity; through incredible good luck and propitious timing he became President of the United States; through his innate sense of humanity and his particularly American grain of humor he touched the common working people; through the power of intellect and persuasive leadership he formulated solutions to slavery and the Union; and through tragic necessity he was assassinated. These were the ingredients for myth, and their common denominators were the strengths and tragedies of democracy on the frontier. This is what Ford and his screenwriter, Lamar Trotti, envisioned to be the Lincoln myth. To give the myth more force and freshness they needed to humanize their symbol, so they told the story of *young* Mr. Lincoln—in other words, both Abe and Mr. Lincoln.

This aspect of the film leads us directly into a confrontation with the monumental and stimulating essay on *Young Mr. Lincoln* compiled by the editors of *Cahiers du Cinéma*. One of their basic arguments was that by depicting Lincoln's youth and mythologizing it, the film repressed politics in favor of morality: "under the idealist mask of Morality [the concealment of politics] has the effect of regilding the cause of Capital with the gold of myth, by manifesting the 'spirituality' in which American Capitalism believes it finds its origins and sees its eternal justification."[8] By never mentioning the basis on which Lincoln gained his fame, "his struggle against the Slaver States," the film "castrated" him of his historico-political dimension, thereby reinforcing the idealization of the myth.[9] In what is otherwise one of the landmarks of semiotic *explication du texte*, this argument is misdirected and actually beside the point. What these French, Marxist-oriented editors failed to see is that the film's ideology is rooted in democracy, not capitalism, nor even republicanism. They simply misunderstood the reality of American politics, which is always idealistic and moralistic. American presidents are intended to be above political ideology. In fact, they are elected because the American public expects them to provide moral leadership by rekindling their faith in the ideals of the myth of American democracy. It is one thing to fault Americans for not scrutinizing their politicians' ideologies—although both get what they deserve— but quite another to attack the premises of a film that accurately portrays the state of American political reality.

This European ideological perspective appears again when the *Cahiers* editors state that Zanuck's interest in this film was motivated by his belief that he was contributing to "the Republican offensive" against Franklin Delano Roosevelt's election and New Deal promises. Would the producer who was responsible for *The Grapes of Wrath* in 1941 and *Wilson* in 1944 make a film of Lincoln because he was a Republican? By 1939 Lincoln belonged to Americans, not Republicans; in fact, most Americans would have been hard pressed to identify his party affiliation. Besides, Zanuck could not have hoped for much support from either Trotti or Ford in his quest to turn this film into Republican propaganda. Both were New Deal Democrats in 1939. A few months earlier Ford had made the true villain of *Stagecoach* a Republican banker. The content of Gatewood's political diatribe is no different than Lincoln's maiden political speech on the porch of his country store. And within a year Zanuck allowed the beneficent government camp director in *The Grapes of Wrath* to appear as an F.D.R. look-alike. It would be absurd to believe that in 1939, after years of depression and on the eve of the European war against fascism, Zanuck, Ford, or virtually anyone else would engage in the task of demythologizing Lincoln. Zanuck's primary interest in the project was for its commercial value (what Hollywood studio head's wasn't?). Mythologizing America's most revered values had been a successful commercial strategy throughout the 1930s. Beyond that, Zanuck would have seen movies serving a social, not a political, function during those difficult depression years: bringing Americans together, reminding them of the country's basic ideals, and inspiring confidence in the future. Finally, Zanuck and Ford might well have thought of *Young Mr. Lincoln* as one of the first films to project a war-effort posture. (Though it was released three months before the invasion of Poland, Ford, like Churchill, would have already seen the fascist threat to democracies.) *Young Mr. Lincoln*, much like Frank Capra's *Mr. Smith Goes to Washington* of the same year, portrayed the myth of the American democrat as a way of stregthening America's resolve in its most cherished yet threatened institution, democracy.

Zanuck's, Ford's, and Trotti's strategy was to particularize, concretize, and humanize Lincoln, on the one hand, while mythologizing him on the other. This, of course, was the basic methodology behind all of Ford's romances. But in *Young Mr. Lincoln* each aspect has been heightened. Portraying a legendary figure's shrouded private life intensifies his modest reality, while the elliptical narrative structure and composed Lincolnesque images sharpen his mythic aura. In effect, the film depicts a mythic Lincoln before he had become the mythic Lincoln.

As the editors of *Cahiers* recognized, this film is structured on a binary system that demands a double reading. But there is more to it than choices between "two careers, two pies, two plaintiffs, two defendants."[10] There is the on-screen and offscreen presence, the daylight beginning and darkened conclusion, the natural gestures and mythic poses, the spirit and letter of the law, natural and human law, and many others. This is Ford's most successful allegory because every level of its double reading is credible. At the human level, Lincoln's youthful private world is one we have never seen before. At the other extreme, Lincoln's story standing for America's frontier development is brilliantly consistent: a primitive and awkward country discovers the importance of law; cut off from its past and choosing independence, it struggles to make its laws work; later, showing its strength, celebrating its birthdays, confronting the irrational forces of mob rule, and embroiled in trials where truth and innocence are at stake, it finally wins the battle of democracy.

The poem carved in marble begins this process of double reading. It serves as the mythic prologue Ford was to use so often during these pre-World War II years. Yet that poem, based on questions his mother would ask of her son, humanizes Lincoln. This dichotomy also establishes the film's on-screen/offscreen structure.[11] The questions are asked by a mother who is never on-screen, about a famous man who is actually never on-screen either. These offscreen elements invest this shy, awkward bumpkin with much of his mythic dimension. This strategy not only humanizes the myth, but serves to reinforce the allegory of America in its pre-Civil War innocence (Lincoln's story) and America in its pre-World War II innocence (America's story). In both instances the film looks toward Lincoln's and America's (offscreen) loss of innocence.

Lincoln's maiden political speech solidifies the film's allegorical mission: Lincoln's and America's discovery of the law and what it means. Leaning back with his feet up on the rail, Lincoln casually comes into view—no mythic Lincolnesque pose here, just Ford's archetypal gesture of America's casual self-confidence. Lincoln is reading. But his stiff, mechanical recitation of political ideology makes it clear that he is not ready to wear the mantle of the American democrat. He has not yet discovered Blackstone, has not lost Ann Rutledge, and has no experience in either mediation or the deeper implications of the law. He represents a wilderness America without its Constitution or Declaration of Independence. When he first discovers the law, he underestimates its human and moral complexity: "Law!" he says, "The right to acquire and hold property, the right to life and reputation, and wrongs are a violation of those right . . . that's all there is to it—right and wrong." Only later during the trial of the two brothers for murder will Lincoln articulate the human and legal relationship between law and morality. When the prosecutor is browbeating the distraught mother, driving her to reveal which of her sons is the murderer Lincoln forces a halt to this legal inhumanity by stating, "I may not know so much of the law, Mr. Prosecutor, but I know what's right and what's wrong." In the first instance, with the confidence of youthful ignorance he sees only the letter of the law. Later, with a humility before the law he understands the human, moral, and ethical dimensions of the law's spirit. Only by experiencing Ann Rutledge's death and thus his loss of innocence could he defend the spirit of the law.

Young Mr. Lincoln, to a great extent, is a celebration of the loss of innocence. This young Lincoln is both the American Adam and the American democrat. But the film is not a tale of Eden because Ford showed that only through the tragedy of the loss of innocence could Lincoln and America mature. Ford made sure that the film's one scene with Ann was clearly Edenic so that it becomes the index by which we measure the future's loss and progress. All the signifiers of this scene indicated a movement back in time. Classical Hollywood film coding (for which Ford was significantly responsible) used left-to-right movement, particularly at a diagonal toward the background of the frame, to indicate progression into the future, whereas the reverse, right-to-left movement, described a return to the past. During their Edenic scene together Ann and Abe walked along the river from right to left (the past); after Ann dies, Lincoln repeats this journey, and when he goes out onto the balcony with Mary Todd to give Ann one last thought, he looks out toward the left at the river. On his way to Mrs. Clay's (his surrogate mother) cabin he and his Sancho Panza, Efe Turner (Eddie Collins), return along the river in the same right-to-left direction. These are all metaphorical journeys into his Edenic past. On the other hand, when he rides his mule into Springfield, sits back-lit in the courtroom, or follows the road to the stormy top of the hill at the film's end, he is shown in left-to-right (the future) positions or movements following his Lincolnesque destiny. Finally, there are the eternal "Lincoln Memorial" poses. These are expressed by frontal shots freezing him in time. This film, then, has a carefully structured mythic choreography: movement right to left back toward an Edenic past; movement left to right toward a Lincolnesque destiny; and static, frontal one-shots memorializing the legendary public images.

The mythical level of the film is further reinforced by the symbolism of Eden. For instance, when Ann interrupts Abe's solitary meditation on the law, he is lying in a field next to the river with his legs up against a huge oak. Law and nature have become intimately connected through the mise-en-scène. Lincoln and the law become one with the tree of life, knowledge, and cosmos. The tree, of course, receives its nourishment from the river, and the river, so closely associated with Ann, adheres to the traditionally ambivalent symbolism of fertility and loss. Ann bequeaths life and destiny to Lincoln at the same time that her death, visually tied to the river, signifies loss through the irreversible passage of time. The river, the tree, and the land cleave to Lincoln as he reads the law. Eventually he will learn that moral law is natural law. This Edenic setting with its resonant symbolism will have planted the seeds of Lincoln's mythic origins.

As Abe and Ann walk along the river, a wooden fence runs between them and the camera—as though the fence (Ford's recurrent indexical signifier of the frontier) separates them from a oneness with nature. Finally, though, they reach an opening in the fence, and there they stand in a moment of natural harmony, having made their journey back through time; there is no fence, a branch makes an arch over them, and the river flows behind them. In this Edenic scene they express their love for each other. Then Ann disappears through the fence opening, leaving Lincoln stranded and isolated behind the fence. The lighting that had been warm and open begins to darken. Lincoln throws a pebble into the river and the widening circles dissolve into an ice floe. The progressions from light to darkness, summer to winter, and stasis to movement all symbolize Lincoln's passage out of Eden and onto America's frontier. The entire texture of the film changes at this point: Abe's casual open-throated dress is replaced by the Lincolnesque tails, top hat, and tie; the camera takes more extreme angles of vision; the mise-en-scène becomes more rigidly composed, the lighting darker and more expressionistically stylized.

Ford and Trotti carefully constructed the symbolism of the next scene to indicate both death and hope. Ford's films always expressed a belief in both cycles and continuity, so the natural symbols of this film are entirely appropriate. It is winter, and Lincoln returns along the same path he had walked with Ann—alone now with an axe, not a basket of flowers. But the ice is breaking up, flowers are poking through the snow, and Lincoln is ready for new beginnings. One cycle is complete: innocence, death, and rebirth. From the beginning of the film Lincoln has been immersed in the elemental aspects of continuous life. He is now ready to confront reality and make his mark as the frontier's mediator.

He confronts those who would exploit democracy's opportunities for freedom. The problem he faces is the frontier's delicate balance between individual freedoms and social controls. This dilemma tests Lincoln's powers of reason and persuasion, as it must all leaders of democracy. The *Cahiers* editors took exception to the "excessive violence of the characterization of Lincoln."[12] Again, these European editors have missed Ford's fundamental point, which is that only the *threat* of violence is able to neutralize the actual violence of frontier democracies. Lincoln simply exercises his reputation for physical strength; he *never* resorts to violence itself. The filmmakers were cognizant of a frontier democracy's potential for violence (from the forces of good as well as evil). This becomes one of the major themes of Ford's

Lincoln (Henry Fonda) and Ann Rutledge (Pauline Moore) walk toward the past (top); Lincoln heads toward the future (bottom).

Lincoln frozen in a Lincolnesque pose (top); Ann leaves Eden heading toward the past as Lincoln stands half turned toward the future (bottom).

post-World War II Westerns. So, the central narrative events in *Young Mr. Lincoln*, a murder and a trial, are not simply commercially added hooks. Two obviously innocent young men are accused of murdering a popular roustabout bully, a mob wants to lynch them, and a trial takes place. Finally, Lincoln extracts a confession from the real murderer, a deputy and friend of the victim. This is the stuff of frontier democracies: violence and the search for order. Lincoln is the American democrat *par excellence*, because his mythical powers are so great and his belief in democracy so strong that he need not resort to violence. Ford's Lincoln understands that American democracy exists only because there were those willing to fight and die for it. That is why the Independence Day parade holds such special meaning for Lincoln. It is his chance to pay tribute to the veterans of wars for democracy. He respectfully doffs his hat to the doddering old veterans of the Revolution. (Ford's caginess is at its best here because he presents the veterans as potential objects of ridicule—then has Lincoln recognize their worth.)

This unobtrusive but important moment is sandwiched in between two essential scenes of Lincoln's mediating powers: the two Mormon antagonists and the pie-baking contest. In the scene between the two Mormons the film mocks the false piety of their Christian brotherhood. One owes the other money and the second has beaten up the first for not paying back the debt. From his archetypal position (feet up on the desk) Lincoln proposes a reasonable solution. But the two Mormons balk. Lincoln then rises from his casual, almost horizontal position. As he does so, the camera remains at the low angle of his former position, so that now he towers into the frame. He stands between them and asks if they have ever heard the story of the time when he butted two men's heads together during the Blackhawk Wars. The two antagonists quickly accept his reasonable solution.

Bill Nichols makes an interesting point in his article, "Style, Grammar, and the Movies," when he notes that there are really two separate legal issues involved: a civil matter, the debt, and a criminal offense, assault and battery. Nichols believes that Lincoln is "subverting the law" by equating these two distinct legal offenses.[13] And further, that Lincoln continually subverts the law "in the name of the Family." This is the same kind of narrow, literal reading of the law that the *Cahiers* editors gave to politics. Ford or Trotti, had they been aware of the two legal issues here, would have answered that it is precisely that kind of legalistic rigidity that has made civilization dangerous, inhuman, and unlivable. Democracy was at its zenith when laws were made and enforced by human pragmatism. On the frontier (not in the wilderness and not in civilization) sensible, viable, humane solutions were achieved by a perfect blending of laws, force, flexibility, and mediation. On the frontier legalistic distinctions were inappropriate (we are carefully reminded that this is the frontier by a prominent placard carried during the parade that reads, "Illinois, Heart of the West"). In fact, in Ford's films legalisms subvert the spirit of the law.

Later, following the Mormon argument and the parade, Lincoln finds himself the judge of a pie-baking contest. Here a solution is more difficult. And through the magic of cinema Lincoln is absolved from choosing. The July Fourth celebration ends on a fade-out, with Lincoln standing between two pieces of pie, mumbling, "So it goes, first one, then the other." He has maintained his aura as the mythic mediator.

But the two greatest tests of democracy are still to come: Can the two accused brothers get a fair trial and can the truth emerge from this process? The fair trial by one's peers has always been democracy's most dramatic symbol, while the lynch mob has remained its most explosive enemy. Fritz Lang, who escaped one form of fascism in Germany, found it again in the lynch mobs of America (*Fury*, 1936). And Mervyn LeRoy, who tried to film the many guises of American fascism in *Little Caesar* and *I Am a Fugitive from a Chain Gang*, made a lynch mob film in 1937, *They Won't Forget*. During the war William Wellman's *Ox Bow Incident* (1943) used the Western as a vehicle for a democracy-versus-lynch mob confrontation. That trend continued past the post-World War II Western and into the anti-McCarthy Westerns. *Young Mr. Lincoln* is one of the central films in this lynch mob subgenre. Later in his career Ford further confronted democracy's two greatest challenges: the unlimited authorized power of *Fort Apache's* Lt. Col. Owen Thursday (Henry Fonda) and the unchecked individual freedom of Liberty Valance (Lee Marvin). Lynch mobs draw these abuses together, so Ford and Trotti make the lynch mob scene the pivotal event of *Young Mr. Lincoln*. It was the frontier that tested America's commitment to democracy and it was the lynch mob that tested the survival of both the frontier and democracy.

The first half of the film establishes Lincoln as the mythic mediator of frontier democracy, while the second half, the trial, measures his powers. But it is during the transitional scene when Lincoln confronts the mob at the jailhouse door that he first understands the power he possesses to shape his destiny. This scene is the film's most dramatic, with sharp key lighting, variety of camera angles, and brilliantly structured speech. The mob forms, but suddenly, as though from nowhere, this intense, powerful, tall god parts the crowd as he heads directly toward the camera (involving the audience as members of the mob). His expression makes it clear that they have angered the forbidding god, that they have defiled his sacred mission. First he challenges them physically, drawing on his reputation and his willingness to fight their strongest member. Then he softens. No longer the wrathful Jehovah, Lincoln becomes a New Testament Christ appealing to the mob through Christian goodness. His speech contains a variety of legal codes: natural law, biblical law—both Old Testament and New Testament, frontier law, American law, and both the spirit and the letter of these laws. These are the laws that comprise American democracy. Lincoln confronts, cajoles, entertains, and persuades the mob to disperse. Standing between them and the jail, he mediates a solution between the forces of fascism (the mob) and the orderly process of civilized democracy (safe incarceration and trial). Finally, he is left standing alone at the doorway, the lonely outsider.

The trial's function has less to do with justifying the outcome of the legal system, than of showcasing the positive qualities of an open frontier democracy: the jury is open to the town drunkard (Francis Ford); the prosecution's elitism, dandyism, and legalisms are constantly debunked; the mother's testimony is a triumph of compassion over legalism; the final confession is elicited through caginess and sagacity; and the farmer's almanac confirms Lincoln as the apotheosis of Truth. Finally, Lincoln's emergence into the light to face "the people" (not visible, thus universal) is nothing less than the fusion of a god with his cosmos. Lincoln has become *the* American democrat of the American frontier.

Drums along the Mohawk: The American Agrarian

Drums Along the Mohawk is a most curious case because, though it was a Zanuck/Twentieth Century-Fox showpiece and has all the mythic resonances of Ford's other 1939 films, it has been largely ignored or dismissed by Ford scholars and film aficionados. Zanuck bought the rights to Walter Edmond's historical novel even before it went into circulation in 1936. Twentieth Century-Fox under Zanuck had strongly supported lavish and well-appointed historical dramas. But Zanuck waited to see how the novel sold before committing himself to the project. Not until 1939 when the novel was in its thirty-first printing and had been a perennial on the bestseller lists did Zanuck decide to film *Drums along the Mohawk.* He then decided to film it in color, which meant that it was to be a studio flagship film. As a result, he scrupulously supervised the screenplay's many treatments (which even included a William Faulkner version). He refused to allow the novel's historical content to dominate the screenplay. For instance, in one of the many lengthy memos he wrote about the script he insisted that "we do not want to make a picture portraying the revolution in the Mohawk Valley."[14] Zanuck's assistant, speaking for him, put it even more bluntly: "We must not let ourselves be bound by the contents of the book—but simply retain the *spirit* of the book. We must concen-

trate our drama, tighten what plot we have and make it more forceful—
so that we build and build to a big sock climax where we let everything
go with a bang. So long as we capture the general line, the characters,
the period—we can and should forget the book."[15] These instructions
amount to the basic principles of Hollywood adaptation. Ford was to
establish himself as one of cinema's great adapters in the 1940s.

Zanuck, Ford, and their screenwriters developed a strategy that was
to become the trademark of all of Ford's filmed adaptations—whether
or not he was directing for Zanuck: (1) condense and cut ruthlessly; (2)
eliminate all but two or three major characters; (3) retain only those
secondary characters whose potential for sharp, quick, comic, or folk
characterization is undeniable; (4) preserve only the essence of human
interaction; (5) eliminate all subplots; (6) restructure the plot for direct
forward action: (7)retain only those scenes that are essential to the new
narrative line, have important dialogue, can be visually expressed, and
are rich in human drama; (8) develop clear narrative or thematic transitions to bridge new gaps; (9) invent scenes, characters, dialogue, and
narrative devices; (10) rearrange and fuse scenes, dialogue, and characters. The basic approach toward the original literary work was to
capture its essence, without ever being intimidated by it.

The script for *Drums* had been evolving for over two years before
Ford was brought in to film it. Though Ford was not intimately involved in the script's process, he did affect its final form. No one can
say to what extent writers are influenced by their knowledge that a
certain director will film their script. Suffice it to say that both Sonya
Levien and Lamar Trotti had recently written scripts for Ford, Trotti
working with him on *Young Mr. Lincoln*. When Ford was free to shoot
Drums, he and Zanuck still found enough changes in the "final" script
to fill a seven-page memo. And finally, even on location Ford was not
satisfied. He wrote this memo to the studio chief: "It is a pictorial story
dealing with two people against the background of the revolution. I
wonder sometimes if we have hit it perfectly in the script. I feel that
when we return there will be adjustments to be made. Your letters
and wires about tempo frighten me. Both the script and the story call
for a placid, pastoral, simple movement which suddenly breaks into
quick, heavy, dramatic overtones. All this requires care."[16] Ford saw
the dilemma the script posed to genre expectations. Either they would
have to be suspended or confounded because the film would have to
be both a Western outside its mythic boundaries and a national chron-
icle centered on an earnest young couple.

Drums along the Mohawk is by no means a mediocre picture. It is,
I believe, one of Ford's most underrated films. Audiences of the day
seemed to agree; it was a commercial success, but it has suffered critically, both in 1939 and since. The film endows the American Revolu-

tion with more mythical significance than it can bear in this culture. The Revolution as a foundation myth has never achieved the imaginative and archetypal force of the West. *Drums* lacked what *Young Mr. Lincoln*, also a non-Western, did not—a powerful mythic hero. Instead, its values are democratically communal, its subjects modestly domestic, and its atmosphere pastorally remote. These are not the qualities that stir the visceral juices of hardened film critics. The film's unmasked national idealism did not help its reputation among skeptical rationalists. *Stagecoach* hid this quality behind the apparently depoliticized and denationalized Western mythos, while Ringo's vengeance quest camouflaged his own domestically pastoral ideal. And though *Young Mr. Lincoln* is an unsuppressed hymn to national idealism, the hero's past loss of innocence and future tragedies harden him into a pragmatic mediator. There are no such countervalences in *Drums along the Mohawk*. As a result it is taken as too innocently idealistic, too earnestly domestic, too placidly pastoral, and too esoterically remote.

The fact is that in an unspectacular fashion *Drums* is a film that cuts across the grain. It maintained naturalistic control over the usually garish tones of 1939 Technicolor. It presents an advanced and sophisticated point-of-view structure that offers a woman's perspective of the frontier. And instead of creating the heroic myth of the American democrat, it expresses the myth of American agrarianism, which does not need a hero cut from the same cloth as the Western. The American yeoman is a more modest figure.

Young Mr. Lincoln portrayed a democracy unconcerned with the concept of free land. Lincoln emerged as the single heroic savior of a more civilized, hence disintegrating and fragmenting democracy. The historian, Turner, believed that free land was the basis of social and economic equality and that agricultural communities, then, were the quintessence of democracy. "American democracy was born of no theorist's dream; it was not carried in the *Susan Constant* to Virginia, nor in the *Mayflower* to Plymouth. It came stark and strong and full of life out of the American forest, and it gained strength each time it touched a new frontier."[17] *Drums along the Mohawk* is about this first stage of democracy, and perhaps the film's failure to generate tension lies in Turner's insight. Democracy's increasing strength was born of each frontier's challenge to that democracy. In *Drums* it is not tested. Instead, the film is a celebration of pluralistic, agrarian, communal democracy. By extolling this form of democracy through its rituals, juxtaposed elemental events, and antinomic values, *Drums* raises American frontier agrarianism to the level of myth.

The film opens on Gil's (Henry Fonda) and Lana's (Claudette Colbert) wedding at the Borst home, which accentuates Lana's civilized background better than a church. The home's mise-en-scène is drenched in rich eighteenth-century European iconography: furnishings, paintings, chamber music, dress, wigs, symmetry, order, and formality. Claudette Colbert's comely Europeanness is in sharp contrast to Henry Fonda's lanky, rawboned Americanness. A covered wagon and a cow stand waiting outside this substantial Albany home. The groundwork for the distinct cultural contrasts between Albany and the Mohawk Valley and Gil and Lana has been carefully prepared by the screenwriters, for no such delineations between civilization and wilderness, Europe and America, East and West exist in the novel.

In quite a striking departure from Hollywood narrative technique this film develops a subjective point-of-view structure and, even more surprising, situates it in the perceptions of Lana. It was probably Sonya Levien who was responsible for this innovation. She wrote the body of the final screenplay, including, for point-of-view purposes, the essential shot and camera-angle instructions. For Ford this no doubt came as a surprise. His established classical style would be at odds with a subjective point-of-view structure. But with Henry Fonda as a more commanding screen presence in the usually male-dominated frontier setting, this point-of-view device created a means by which both characters could achieve equal weight, thereby redirecting the film's emphasis from individual male heroics to a familial center more in line with the realities of its agrarian subject. The wedding scene, then, establishes the cultural shock awaiting Lana in the wilderness. Once beyond her parents' safe, civilized compound, the film becomes immersed in Lana's actual line of vision, as she sees things clearly, distortedly, and ambiguously. The film is almost a kind of *bildungscinema* where Lana grows into womanhood through the trials she encounters and the way she perceives them. And it is this aspect of the film that is most often misunderstood by critics who complain that, as Andrew Sarris put it, "the film never recovers from Claudette Colbert's whining at the outset of her ordeal in the wilderness."[18]

As the covered wagon leaves the Borst compound, Lana reacts to the wilderness with naive enthusiasm: "This is the most beautiful country I've ever seen." Soon this "beautiful country" becomes storm-laden and infested with flies. When they arrive at the cabin in the middle of the storm, it appears small, forlorn, and empty to Lana. Inside the cabin the camera follows and crosscuts between Lana and her bewildered, disappointed perceptions. When she looks up at the sleeping loft, the high-angle shot intensifies her smallness; when she looks at her new home, the darkness intensifies its smallness. Sensing her concern, Gil offers his consoling point of view: "It looks so fine to me because I built it. I didn't realize it might look different to a girl who had been raised in a big house like yours. I'll put up the mare and we'll get something to eat and you'll feel warm. Things will look different then." The wedding, which had engraved Lana's lifestyle on our minds, becomes the explicit frame of reference now. Space, large or small, dark or light, rich or poor, is measured by point of view, context, and light.

When Gil leaves, Ford indulges in a Kuleshov experiment to prove this point. Lana turns around and sees through the flickering darkness the face of an Indian in the doorway. Given the situation and our involvement in Lana's point of view, the Indian appears menacing. As the Indian approaches, she screams hysterically. Gil runs into the cabin, there to greet, not a bloodthirsty savage, but his old friend, Blue Back (Chief Big Tree). Gil calms Lana down and Blue Back leaves. As Gil holds Lana, she looks again at the door and sees that Blue Back has returned. The shot Ford uses at this moment is precisely the same shot he used earlier to frighten Lana—and the audience. Now, however, the syntagmatic context and the psychological perspective have changed. Ford has used the Russian principle of montage to effectively involve us in Lana's changing mental state. Ford will make further use of Blue Back in ambiguous contexts to force the audience to question its racial assumptions reinforced through years of movie watching and historical stereotyping. Lana will continue to mature, though her role as the center of the film's point of view will diminish.

Instead of filming the Battle of Oriskany, the filmmakers have Gil describe his part in it. Cynics may scoff, believing that Ford and Zanuck only wished to save money. Even so, that narrative technique becomes an organic part of the film's design, allowing Lana to share Gil's experiences. His half-delirious monologue is a brilliant piece of descriptive writing and stands as an early example of the imaginative power of linguistic imagery in film.

While Lana is being forced to see and adapt to her world clearly and realistically, Gil, already the frontiersman, has become the dreamer, the visionary. When they first settle on their land, Gil stops haying for a moment to lean on his scythe and dream out over the Mohawk Valley. Lana tries to enter his world, but he doesn't hear her. Then he describes their future home and land. The audience supplies his inner vision of the civilizing of the wilderness. What Gil envisions is America, neither a wilderness nor a small plot of land west of Albany during the American Revolution. He sees America's future. For Ford, Fonda's character had always been involved in the great movements of American history. His clear, translucent gaze defines Ford's pragmatic visionaries: Gil Martin, Abe Lincoln, Tom Joad, and Wyatt Earp. Before Lana can enter his world, she must fully experience the wilderness. Later when Gil marches to battle in his minuteman garb, Lana stands on a hill watching the columns of men file off into the distance. She shades her eyes, as though she too is beginning to envision the march of history. By the end of the film, when they watch the raising of the American flag over their fort, they see together what in essence they had earlier envisioned separately, the emergence of a nation.

Out of these personal and public images of history are founded the deeper resonances of myth. Ford, Zanuck, and the screenwriters took great care to immerse this film in the objects, people, and rituals of mythic America. For instance, fireplaces have always signified the warmth of the home and the union of man and woman. In a number of Ford films they become symbols for familial civilization: *Drums along the Mohawk, The Quiet Man, The Searchers*. In *Drums* the fireplace becomes an indexical motif that establishes the extent of Gil's and Lana's stability. It also contributes to the visual and psychological atmosphere of each space. When Lana first enters her new home, that tiny bleak cabin, there is no fire in the hearth (in the novel, by contrast, there is). The cabin's cold grimness contributes to her first fearful reaction to Blue Back. Gil then tells her that things will look different after he has built a fire. And they do. The cabin suddenly becomes inviting and Blue Back no longer appears frightening. When this cabin has been burned to the ground by the Indians and the white provocateur, Gil and Lana return to the charred remains in a gentle snowstorm. What is left standing (symbolically, as well as realistically) is the fireplace and the chimney. Just as the winter and the charred ruins signal the end of one era, so the mortared strength of the hearth keeps a vestige of their dream alive as they stand together in front of it. In a sense, what burned was the end of Lana's link with her Europeanized past, for in the scorched timbers she finds the broken shards of the sugar bowl her mother had given her. Then, with the deliberate care of a woman packing away her past, she replaces them in the ruins (presaging Ma Joad's memento-in-the-fire scene).

Lana and Gil accept a job working for a widow, Mrs. McKlennar (Edna May Oliver). Lana's newfound frontier pragmatism, now that she has broken with her past, enables her to sooth Gil's wounded frontier agrarian pride at having to work for someone else. After Mrs. McKlennar shows them the house they will live in, they sit in front of an unused, corncob-filled fireplace. Though it is cold and cheerless, Lana says, "It's a beautiful fireplace." Later in the film Ford will show us the same hearth in an almost unrecognizable setting: a warm fire, a mother and child, rocking chairs, musket, and kettles. In *Drums along the Mohawk* the hearth acts as the primary indexical signifier of Gil's and Lana's American dream: to carve out of the wilderness a frontier home and a productive farm. Though the final fireplace shot indicates that they have achieved their dream, it is not enough. The concluding shots suggest that they must also work to create a community and even a nation out of this wilderness.

Through careful casting, directing, and costuming of a host of deep-seated American folk types, Ford, as he had in *Stagecoach*, deepened the mythic iconography. He demanded that his screenwriters have a good colloquial ear, though he and his character actors often contributed bits of salty dialogue themselves. Ford's affection for these fictional characters must have grown out of his personal affinity for colorful folk types. He always hired and surrounded himself with serendipitous actors and stuntmen—the Hollywood drifters, the people who had wandered into the land of tinsel from ranches, farms, merchant ships, etc. They looked like folk types because they were folk types. Ford simply capitalized on their inherent qualities by reserving his films' most pungent, flavorful, and comic dialogue for these vernacular types. His reading of history, affinity for remote places, and access to research staffs reinforced his natural inclination to portray folk characters accurately. A number of his favorite character actors appear in *Drums along the Mohawk* at their archetypal best: John Carradine as Caldwell, the spectre-thin, treasonous *agent provocateur*; Arthur Shields as a minister with the rectitude of a Puritan preacher, the entrepreneurial sense of a fabric salesman, and the militarism of a fort defender; Ward Bond as the hearty, good-time-Charlie; Russell Simpson as the perennially stolid doctor; Roger Imhof as General Herkimer, the rotund, kindly, immigrant father figure; Jack Pennick as the perpetual sergeant-at-arms type; Si Jenks as the tiny, bearded, tobacco-chewing idiot savant; and, of course, Francis Ford as the drunken, coonskin-capped fool from the hills. And, in her only appearance in a Ford film, Edna May Oliver created another of her scene-stealing performances as the tough-as-nails widow with the heart of gold.

Since every mythos is a world unto itself, it must be peopled with those types who can recognizably fill out the full range of its community. Through their comic qualities, precise functions, and geographical rootedness these folk types humanize the serious, abstract, and rootless knights of mythic romances. But the knights of romance are never quite as serious, abstract, and rootless as the kings of epics. Gil (and, yes, Lana) reflects this humanized, civilized, down-to-earth quality more than most Fordian knights. Abe Lincoln acquires a restlessness after Ann Rutledge's death; Tom Joad, an outlaw in *The Grapes of Wrath*, leaves the family to search for Casy's holy grail of "the one big soul that belongs to ever'body"; and Wyatt Earp, in *My Darling Clementine*, moves on with only a promise to return. All are involved in the process of civilizing the frontier, but Gil and Lana are more completely a part of their more agrarian community. Gil is not quite the loner that the other three Fonda knights are. He marries, then participates in the ritual of his child's birth. Both are civilizing ceremonies. His knightly accoutrements include the scythe as well as the musket. He and Lana, unified and with family, watch as one half of their holy grail, the flag of democratic unity and independence, is hoisted above the fort, then immediately return to civilize their home and land. The romance looks back on the achievements of the quest and forward to elusive events not yet grasped.

These heroes and folk characters, however, must be supported by archetypal imagery and ritual actions if the myth is to cohere. Cross-stitch Americana sampler titles set the tone during the credits and announce the changes in setting during the early phases of the film. Long establishing shots with metaphoric resonances validate the fusion of the real and the marvelous: the covered wagon passing through the gates of civilization into the wilderness; the wagon framed against the horizon; the encounter with the Edenic flock of sheep; Gil leaning on the haying scythe; the peopled authenticity of the revolutionary fort and the land-clearing ceremony; the perfectly rendered harvest dance; the slanting light through the Mohawk Valley forest; the "Christina's World" poetry of Lana watching the column of army and minutemen march off into the distance; the charred remains of the cabin through the soft winter snowfall; the birth of the Martins' child in the carefully wrought colonial bedroom with the old crones chuckling at the new father's innocent awkwardness; and finally, the raising of the American flag as immigrant, Indian, black, and other settlers pause for a moment in the middle of their work to watch the birth of a nation.

Many of these archetypal images are shots frozen by distance, isolating them from the flow of action and time, thus rendering them timeless. But they return to time through the formalized movements of the film's ceremonies, many having to do with the juxtaposition of life and death, creation and destruction, beginnings and endings. The wedding, of course, is powerfully symbolic of beginnings and endings. But Ford and the screenwriters were not content with just the ritual. They reinforced the power of this cycle through point of view. The first shot of the wagon leaving the Borst compound is from the parents' perspective, i.e., an ending. This shot dissolves into the wagon approaching the camera, i.e., a beginning. This technique of the superimposed moment offers us an instant of timelessness and in the separate shots the cycles of beginnings and endings, past, present, and future. This is the essence of mythmaking in film.

The cycle of creation and destruction is carried out through the symbolic properties of fire. The land-clearing celebration is a community inititation rite where all the neighbors help the newcomer clear his land by chopping and burning, which, from a civilizing point of view, is creative. But they are also destroying the wilderness. It is therefore significant that they are driven out by an Indian attack in the middle of this white man's civilizing ceremony. The Indians redress this ritual by burning the settlers' homes. By destroying the creations of civilization the Indians hope to regenerate their wilderness. The fire motif continues: even though fires in the hearth symbolize civilization's stability, still Mrs. McKlennar, Adam, and Joe Boleo (Francis Ford) are victims of fire's destructiveness. Finally, Gil and Lana begin a new life out of the ashes of their old home.

Lana's miscarriage is triggered by the Indian attack. At the fort Gil must choose between staying with his wife or fighting for this new land. Both are ambiguous life-and/or-death choices. Later, after the Battle of Oriskany there are a series of death and resurrection juxtapositions. Gil, who has been presumed dead, is found by Lana and given new life. Then he describes the death of an Indian who had tried to kill him. This scene was effectively written using the frozen action imagery typical of William Faulkner (who, interestingly enough, wrote absolutely no Faulknerian description into his version of the screenplay). Meanwhile in the next room General Herkimer is dying. In the morning as the sun streams in on Gil, Lana tells him she is going to have a child. At that very moment General Herkimer dies and the minister intones, "I am the resurrection and the light, saith the Lord." The general's body passes in front of the screen momentarily overpowering Gil's and Lana's life-force. This scene fades out and fades in on Gil boiling water (fire as creation) for the birth of their child. Rain and sun, night and morning, death and life reinforce the mythic agrarian rhythms of this sequence.

Ford could not get through this film without a dance. So the birth of Gil's and Lana's child is followed by the quintessential ritual of agrarian America, the harvest dance. No ceremony could be so completely life-affirming: the circularity of the dance signifying the union of community; the celebration of reaping what one sows; the marriage announcement of a young couple. Gil, as is so often the case with the mediating hero, stands outside the circle of dancers, and instead leaves to rock his child—an act that establishes the primacy of the family over the community. Yet this autumn celebration always has a melancholy tinge to it, for it signals the beginning of the end and foreshadows the trials ahead. When Lana sees Gil rocking their child, she sits down and prays: "Please, God, please let it go on like this forever." There is just enough hubris in these words to indicate that the worst is yet to come.

The rest of the film rises to a defending-the-fort climax. When Ford wrote in his memo that the film up until this climax was a "placid pastoral simple movement" he might well have meant this demanded a rhythm of agrarian rituals. The filmmakers envisioned America's birth emerging from the myth of the American frontier and maturing on the myth of American agrarianism. All three of Ford's 1939 films, regardless of how responsible he was for their production, optimistically projected new beginnings for America. They project a cycle of births: in *Stagecoach* the birth of the child in the wilderness propels Ringo and Dallas into a relationship that will (we are led to believe, after the end of the film) result in a new generation in a new world; in *Drums along the Mohawk* we can imagine that Gil and Lana are the couple that will create that new generation, since they represent the domesticated progression of civilization—the birth of their child is followed by the birth of the United States of America; and in *Young Mr. Lincoln* we witness the birth of America's legendary father of democracy and America's rebirth. In these films the heroes and the allegorized America find their source of strength on the frontier. In 1939 Americans searched for and our filmmakers provided the sources for America's strength through various myths of the American dream. Depression had haunted the nation for ten years; war loomed on the horizon. Ford and Zanuck looked to the past for their optimism, to a time when the frontier was very much alive. Ford's next four films before World War II were not quite so sanguine. The frontier was closing fast. Obviously no visionary master plan could exist for a director in the American studio system, but placing *The Grapes of Wrath* and *Tobacco Road* beside *Young Mr. Lincoln* and *Drums along the Mohawk* can have a chilling effect on the dream of the moral value inherent in the progress of America's frontier civilization.

3

The Myth of American Agrarianism: *The Grapes of Wrath* and *Tobacco Road*

THE GRAPES OF WRATH (1940) and *Tobacco Road* (1941), both based on celebrated novels of the 1930s, drove to the heart of a myth crucial to the American dream, American agrarianism. Of the six myths of the American dream discussed in this book—Adam, frontier, democrat, agrarianism, individualism, and civilization—the Jeffersonian ideal of a democracy based upon a nation of small land-owning farmers is possibly the most important because it has been the underdog favorite in America's longest and bitterest debate: Jeffersonian agrarianism versus Hamiltonian capitalism. The American dream began with the land. The earliest accounts of America always emphasized its rich abundance. While there were many reasons for sailing to the New World, the opportunity to acquire and work property of one's own seems to have headed the list. That agrarianism became the credo of a major president and author of the Declaration of Independence gave it the stamp of political power and philosophical credibility. And that this credo became locked in a deadly battle with capitalistic mercantilism endowed it with the energy born of tension.

Jeffersonian agrarianism embodied all of the myths that are at work in the films of John Ford. Certainly it was on the frontier, wherever it lay, that land became available to the common man. Here he could be in his own eyes the first man (Native Americans didn't matter, of course) to cultivate this virgin wilderness. So, this American Adam became the progenitor of American civilization as he attempted to plow the wilderness into a garden. The land gave him worth and dignity, according to the credo, hence empowering him with political equality and endowing him with individualistic self-esteem. It was his land to do with as he pleased, to work it as he saw fit, and to behave on in any way he wished. This potential for unbridled individualism might have been mitigated by one's inclusion in the democratic community; still, the roots for a special kind of American conflict were also here. At any rate, the dream of American land evolved into a political philosophy, and finally into a myth. And though today this is no longer

The death of American agrarianism: the unused plow in Tobacco Road.

in reality an agrarian nation, the myth lives on in various forms, principally in the desire of most Americans to own their own home or their
own plot of land. Legislation has kept this dream alive because politicians often draw upon the myth to buy off more mercantile legislation.
Despite the fact that more and more Americans live in urbanized tenant situations, the dream persists.

The stories of *The Grapes of Wrath* and *Tobacco Road* are about
both the demise of the agrarian reality and the persistence of the
dream. While the agrarian myth is absolutely central to both novels
and both films, many of Ford's films have agrarianism as at least a pe-
ripheral issue. *Drums along the Mohawk* is the film that reaches deepest into the agrarian myth, depicting a community of yeomen in the
Mohawk Valley during the Revolution. The film is a virtual textbook
on what Henry Nash Smith calls "the yeoman ideal." This yeoman "had
become the hero of a myth . . . a symbol which could be made to bear
an almost unlimited charge of meaning. . . . The career of this symbol
deserves careful attention because it is one of the most tangible things
we mean when we speak of the development of democratic ideas in
the United States."[1] During the revolutionary era nine-tenths of America's white population were yeomen. They were the truly representative citizens of that time.[2] So Henry Fonda as Gil Martin of *Drums* in
his quest to settle himself and his family on a farm on the frontier
represents the first in a long tradition of small, independent agrarian
Americans. In fact, Gil's lowest psychological moment occurs when he
is forced to work someone else's land after the Indians had burned his
house and crops. He has, in effect, been placed in the same tenant-
farmer position as the Joads in *The Grapes of Wrath*.

Between Gil Martin, the colonial yeoman who finally works his own
land, and Tom Joad, the Okie tenant farmer turned outlaw and social
activist, stand a variety of American farmers. It is made clear in *Young
Mr. Lincoln* that, though Abe begins in the film as a storekeeper, his
values are shaped by the farming community from which he sprang. A
farming family provides Lincoln with his law books and later becomes
his surrogate family. So, though Lincoln represents a new stage in the
evolution of civilization, he owes his civilized greatness to his agrarian
roots. This occurred on the pre-Civil-War frontier of Illinois. Further
west and after the Civil War new frontiers drew new farmers, the sod-
busters and homesteaders. It is in the Westerns that farming as a moral
value becomes more complex.

The farmer has rarely been the solitary hero of romances, since he
was not a transient outsider beset by conflicting values. Instead, he has
been portrayed as the backbone of a democratic community—but only
so long as he conformed to the yeoman image. If he becomes the huge
rancher, in the Tom Dunson (John Wayne) mold in *Red River*, he be-

gins to represent the values of the Hamiltonian capitalist. The Jeffersonian ideal is based upon both the modest size and the actual working of farmland. The unequivocally positive heroes of Ford's Western romance, the Ringo Kid of *Stagecoach* and Wyatt Earp of *My Darling Clementine*, both settle down at the end of each film. Ringo says to Dallas, "I still got a ranch across the Border—it's a nice place, a real nice place—trees, grass, water—there's a cabin half-built. A man could live there and a woman. Will you go?" Though Ringo calls it a ranch, his pastoral description of it and an implication of modest size predict a yeoman's future for them. Perhaps this was a calculated ambiguity aimed at mediation by the screenwriter. In *Clementine* Wyatt's transformation on the dance floor of the half-furnished church occurs through his acceptance into a community of farmers, who just moments earlier have been shown pouring into Tombstone. As with Lincoln, Wyatt will not become a farmer, but his community support will come from them. *The Searchers* presents a more complex picture of farming. Ethan and Aaron Edwards (John Wayne and Walter Coy) are brothers. Ethan is the wandering outsider who has lost his true love to his frugal, sodbusting brother. Neither is very sympathetically portrayed. Aaron's role consigns him to dull oblivion and death, while Ethan, shut out of the Jorgensen's homestead, is condemned to wander forever in the wilderness. Mrs. Jorgensen (Olive Carey) describes a Texican (a Texas Territory homesteader) as "nothin' but a human man way out on a limb." She sees them as mere links in the evolution of progress because "someday this country's goin' to be a fine, good place to be." In Ford's films the primacy of the family means that Ethan cannot leave a legacy for that evolution. Ethan is the progenitor of the childless Tom Doniphon (John Wayne) in *The Man Who Shot Liberty Valance*. Doniphon has gone so far as to try small ranching, but time has passed him by. Tom Doniphon is, in turn, the progenitor of Tom Joad. Their agrarianism has been lost to an urban "progress" Mrs. Jorgensen of *The Searchers* never envisioned. This evolution is described by the editor of the local newspaper at the Territorial convention in *Liberty Valance*:

"And then with the Westward march of our nation came the pioneer and the buffalo hunters, the adventurous and the bold. And the boldest of these were the cattlemen who seized the wide open range for their own personal domain, and their law was the law of the hired gun. Now, today have come the railroad and the people, the steady, hard-working citizens, the homesteader, the shopkeeper, the builder of cities."

Though agrarianism may be waning in the West, the editor believes that the small, independent entrepreneurs may be able to keep democracy alive.

In *The Grapes of Wrath* and *Tobacco Road*, however, the Joads and
the Lesters are tenant farmers and sharecroppers who own nothing.
Making the dream of land ownership come true has slipped from their
grasp. They now work for large-scale, impersonal, absentee landlords.
Such agribusiness represents the antithesis of Jeffersonian agrarianism,
and it is anathema to all of Ford's values. These values espouse the
natural rights of labor over the legal rights of contracts. According to
this theory, the Joads and the Lesters may claim ownership of the land
they and their ancestors have worked. The forces lined up against
these families would use the land for speculation or industrial capitalism (euphemized in both films as "scientific cultivation") so that the
land would no longer be used naturally nor worked individually. Its
spiritual value would be lost. The machine would enter the garden,
destroying in its wake individualism and democracy. The question that
is never raised in any of these films, however, is, did not the very
dream of turning the wilderness into a garden represent a vision of
progress that would inevitably lead to the destruction of the garden?
That is, since the simple plow is a machine, the machine entered the
garden the moment it broke open the land. Therefore, the belief in
progress led the agrarians into the hands of the mercantile capitalists.
The situations presented by *The Grapes of Wrath* and *Tobacco Road*
were inevitable.

The Grapes of Wrath (1940)

Both films, but *The Grapes of Wrath* in particular, take as their subject the nightmare of the wasteland and the dream of fertility. This
should not be surprising given John Steinbeck's well-known interest in
romance. From the beginning this story was conceived of as the quest
of a human-sized deliverer, Tom Joad, who must fight the monster,
which is, as Northrop Frye puts it, "the sterility of the land itself."[3]
Steinbeck, as Chester Eisinger pointed out, wrote the novel fully
aware that the Jeffersonian ideal had failed.[4] The yoking of romance
and agrarianism drove the novel deep into the archetypal consciousness of American culture. And, as we have seen, this combination
made the marriage of *The Grapes of Wrath* to John Ford a natural,
since Ford was a romancer who had in the past and would in the future
express the Jeffersonian ideal in many of his films.

There were also practical and commercial reasons for the marriage.
Zanuck purchased the rights to this explosive novel within a month of
its publication in March 1939. The film would be released less than
one year later—an extraordinarily short time for such a major film,
even by Hollywood assembly-line standards. Nunnally Johnson, who
had written the script for Ford and Zanuck on *The Prisoner of Island*

in 1936, was assigned to write *Grapes*, and later *Tobacco Road*. Johnson was a conservative Southerner, so it would seem natural for him to de-emphasize Steinbeck's specific left-wing arguments. Johnson has justified his method, saying that, "I thought the politics were secondary to the story of the Joads."⁵ It turns out, of course, that this is the major issue in the novel-into-film controversy. There were those who advised Zanuck to buy the rights but not shoot the film, thereby suppressing an inflammatory project. Certainly, as a product of the Hollywood mainstream, he would never have allowed an overt expression of Steinbeck's leftist finger-pointing. And, in fact, Zanuck himself decided to flesh out and highlight the now-famous "We're the people" speech by Ma Joad (Jane Darwell) by placing its optimistic survival message at the end of the film. The real question is, did Zanuck, Johnson, and Ford pervert or subvert the novel's essence and message? One answer is that Steinbeck admired the film; another is that many of Steinbeck's attacks make the novel seem dated today, while the film's more universal approach has helped it become a classic. But even more to the point is the fact that the film's retention of the Jeffersonian ideal places it to the left of the Hamiltonian capitalism that drove the Okies off their land. While the film is not so pointed as to the causes of the exploitation, it does not dodge the essential issues of dispossession: corporate ownership, means of ownership, uses of the land, and worker exploitation. While Ma's speech ends the film, Tom's social activist speech precedes it. Two alternatives are posited: plodding survival for some, political action for others.

The film, like the novel, is double-edged. As a romance it suggests the optimism of quest and delivery, and as a film of American agrarianism it faces the reality of the loss of that dream. Though the novel's despair and determinism have been eliminated in the film, they have been replaced with nightmarish imagery of the wasteland. Ford himself was attracted to the story's dualistic themes of dispossession and quest for survival:

"The whole thing appealed to me—being about simple people—and the story was similar to the famine in Ireland, when they threw the people off the land and left them wandering on the roads to starve—part of my Irish tradition—but I like the idea of this family going out and trying to find their way in the world. It was a timely story."⁶

The Grapes of Wrath brings the myth of the frontier full circle. What had once been a wilderness wasteland has now become a civilized wasteland. Progress has sacrificed both the land and those who work it. The myth of the frontier requires that new frontiers be searched for and found. In the American myth California represents the last frontier (before outer space replaced it) as well as the best frontier. Its symbolic value is ambiguous. Though the first shots of it in the film show a dreamlike fertility, they also show barriers to it. And once the Joads encounter California, they discover that the Hamiltonian capitalists have already claimed this last frontier. There is no land left for the agrarians or Ma Joad's "people." For Ma there is nothing left but blind faith in their Darwinian survival. Tom is now an outlaw. (The gangster film was founded upon the premise that gangsters were frontiersmen who had run out of frontiers and were driven to turn inward against the society that delimited their freedom of action and their need for space and solitude.) Tom must now fight society for the survival of "our folks." While critics of the film have derided its ending as a series of simplistic, upbeat homilies, one could just as easily argue that these are the only articles of faith left to them. The American frontiers have been exhausted, big business controls what fertile lands remain, and the once-proud yeomen have been reduced to transient laborers and outlaws. These are the inevitable conclusions that the narrative structure and mise-en-scène of the entire film reach—and they cannot be reversed by two ringing speeches. Seen in this light, Ma's and Tom's words are plaintively illusory, spoken to stave off their own despair, rather than convince the viewers that all is well.

If the end of the film makes it clear that there is no land available to the small farmers, the beginning opens on land, but already it is a vast wasteland. The opening shot places all the weight on the empty power of civilization. The width of the highway dwarfs the sterile land, while the foregrounded telephone poles and wires repeat the highway's crossing pattern. The implements of civilization dominate the mass of the frame, are foregrounded, and imply a North, South, East, and West pervasiveness that stretches beyond the frame. Deep in the background, a puny, lonely figure walks toward us. What land there is is barren and fragmented. Man and the land are clearly diminished in this key opening shot. Add to this its ghostly flat light, eerie effects of the high-contrast film stock, and depersonalized geometry of the composition, and the result is a surrealist dreamscape echoing the images of Salvador Dali or Giorgio de Chirico. The reverberations from T. S. Eliot's *The Waste Land* are also in the mise-en-scène with its "heap of broken images, where the sun beats / And the dead tree gives no shelter." Tom is defined by his "shadow at morning striding behind you," going where "I will show you fear in a handful of dust."[7]

This dreamlike imagery presses deeply into much of the film—and this quality exists in the film alone. For instance, when Tom and Casy (John Carradine) find the Joad shack, it is seen at dusk through a howling dust storm. Like its only inhabitant, Muley (John Qualen), it emerges from the darkness surrounded by a lonely, ghostly aura. Inside, it is completely dark. Tom's family seems to have disappeared. Then a sound, then a disembodied voice, then a shadowy face appears. The scene continues with only a candle flickering, giving Muley and the entire scene a sense of nightmarish, spatial disorientation. The film suggests by the power and centrality of the Muley episode that it is his face and nightmare that motivates the Joads in their quest to keep the agrarian dream alive. When Muley tells his story of how he was driven from the land, the flashback imagery shifts to the daylight dream atmosphere of the film's opening shot with its flat light, long shadows, and spare composition. Dissolves serve as the transitions back and forth into the flashbacks. After Muley is left squatting alone in the dust, after a quick return to the present, a machine montage evokes the forces that drove Muley and the Okies off their land. In this montage the weaker of the two superimposed images is of a caterpillar tread that fills the screen driving toward and over the viewer in one continuous, hypnotic movement. The faded power of this half of the superimposed image create an almost subliminal effect, further deepening the dream quality of this montage. Though this is Muley's nightmare, Ford has designed it to make it ours as well.

Later in the film the lush images of California are presented in a misty distance, always beyond some barrier, as though it is the inaccessible dream of fertility. For instance, what the Joads first see of California is a hazy range of mountains across the Colorado River. Upon seeing it, Pa says with a tone of forced enthusiasm, "There she is, folks, the land of milk and honey—California." They all look at each other in surprised disbelief. Then the morning after they have passed the inspection station and crossed the desert, they finally see the fertile California valley of their dreams. But this time it is across a man-made safety barrier, and the experience is further muted by the announcement of Grandma's death. She had been the final link to their Oklahoma roots. Grandpa had died earlier gripping a handful of native soil. Now upon seeing lush California, Pa acknowledges its dreamed reality, "I never knowed there was anything like her." The film has now established the opposition of nightmarish wastelands and dreamlike fertility.

Immediately, then, the film shifts its attention away from the land. After the fade-out on Tom and Ma looking out over the valley, the Joads push their truck to a gas station, then drive out to a Hooverville camp. Urbanization, poverty, and worker exploitation are California's constants. It is in the Hooverville camp that Casy rediscovers his faith. Early in the film Casy told Tom how he had "lost the spirit" and had "nothin' to preach about no more." This occurs just after the film's opening wasteland imagery. One could argue that the egregious sound-stage quality of the Tom-and-Casy scene actually reinforces the film's death-of-the-land theme. Although we know that it was shot on sound-stages to cloak the controversial project in secrecy, its metaphorical effect is to replace actual land with an artificial backdrop. It is impossible to have faith in such a wasteland, "I just as soon go one way as the other," Casy says to Tom. But in Hooverville Casy finds something to preach about again. A concern for society at large replaces Casy's and Tom's interest in the land and the landed. So while their transformation heralds a new faith in social activism, it also means the end of the agrarian ideal. That dream is dead. When the film's theme song, "The Red River Valley," is played as Tom disappears into the darkness, leaving Ma to mourn their parting, the music is as much an elegy to the land as to the breakup of the family. It was, after all, the land that held the family together. Earlier in the film this same tune had presided over Ma's ritual burning of her past. She burns mementos, but it is the land she mourns. Both of these scenes occur in darkness, not quite as dark as Muley's nightmarishness, but murky enough to suggest the twilight zone of bad dreams. The Red River Valley has disappeared into the darkness of the past.

If the myth of American agrarianism is on the ropes, its sole survivor is embodied in Ma Joad, the film's Earth Mother. Once Ford's initial request to have the gaunt Beulah Bondi play Ma was vetoed by Zanuck, and the warm, rotund Jane Darwell was cast in that role, Ma's characterization shifted from a realistic portrayal to a mythic one. The soil would have hardened Beulah Bondi; it regenerates Jane Darwell. Its depletion would have impoverished the former, while the latter seems sustained by her physical and spiritual abundance. Darwell is like a mound of earth, solid and warm. She identifies herself with the archetypal woman who, she says, sees life as "all one flow, like a stream, little eddies, little waterfalls, but the river it goes right on." She is the agrarian life force by virtue of her symbolic association with the land and water. These symbol clusters are all found in the film's theme song, "The Red River Valley." This factor and the song's presence during Ma's most important scenes makes this her theme song as well. In the face of dispossession and disintegration the Earth Mother holds what's left of the family together and keeps the agrarian dream alive.

But in this world of tenant farmers the dream is all that's left. In Muley's flashback he painfully states the central conflict of land ownership: "And that's what makes it ourn—bein' born on it, an' workin' on it, an' dyin'—dyin' on it. An' not no piece o' paper with writin' on it." What he expresses is, again, a Jeffersonian and Hamiltonian dilemma, natural rights of ownership gained through occupation and labor as opposed to ownership by the right of legal contracts. Ownership of the land one worked is what put the heart in the agrarian ideal. So when Muley is literally bulldozed off the land the combination of legal rights, machinery, and corporate power dramatically signals the victory of Hamiltonian capitalism over Jeffersonian agrarianism. The Okies' experiences in California simply reinforce this fact, and the film never flinches from this conclusion. Tom's and Ma's concluding speeches acknowledge the reality of the Hamiltonian wasteland, while expressing the hope that they can keep the fertile dream of agrarianism alive.

One major problem with agrarianism has been the emphasis it placed on individualism at the expense of collectivism. According to the credo, agrarianism promoted the growth of individual freedom, the moral worth and human dignity gained from individually working one's own land, the acquisition of personal wealth that was not parasitical, and the optimism and assurance that accrues from self-sufficiency and equality. Though the evolution of civilization valued socialization over individualism, on the frontier where this conflict was fought, individualism had always been the sentimental favorite. Collectivist social, political, and economic philosophies have always been considered restrictive, denying individuals the freedoms they believe are embodied in the American dream. This does not prevent them, however, from relying on others as a last resort. Within the balance there are priorities. Again *Drums along the Mohawk* is instructive. There are collective land clearings, harvest dances, child birthing, and fort defenses. Still, these actions are specialized events and communal rituals that stave off complete societal and physical annihilation.

The era of *The Grapes of Wrath* has forced a change in attitude toward collectivization. I would argue that the primary thrust of this film is toward the Joads' shift from family self-sufficiency to societal involvement. Since agrarian individualism has failed to confront adequately the forces of corporate collectivism, the film suggests a kind of humanistic collectivism as an alternative. For instance, both Tom's and Ma's speeches at the end of the film stress their commitment to units larger than the family. Tom says, "An' I been wonderin' if all our folks got together an' yelled—" and "it's like Casy says, a fella ain't got a soul of his own, but only a piece of a big soul—the one big soul that belongs to everybody." Ma's language stresses collective pronouns, "but we keep a-comin'. We're the people that live. Can't nobody wipe us out. Can't nobody lick us. We'll go on forever, Pa. We're the people."

The Joads' progression to this state of societal solidarity is carefully written into the screenplay and woven into the mise-en-scène. The film's first image is of Tom Joad alone, dwarfed by the wasteland. Then he meets Jim Casy, who is also alone and without a congregation. Then Muley's story graphically shows the futility of one family's stand against the forces of commerce. Muley, too, is left alone, reduced to a squatting shadow and a "graveyard ghost." The story continues, focusing only on the Joads as they prepare to leave for California. But when their truck enters the main highway, they slip in among a caravan of other Okies hitting the road. This is the first image of a common plight and a mass movement. Still, the Joads remain essentially isolated and self-reliant. But in California, when the reality begins to replace the dream, the Joads are confronted by their isolation. This occurs at the Hooverville Camp. As their truck enters the camp, a radical departure from Ford's usual omniscient point-of-view camera placement takes place. Suddenly the camera is placed on the truck in such a way that it approximates the Joads' point of view, and this is reinforced by having poverty-stricken camp occupants wander in front of the truck and stare at the camera/Joads/audience. The subjective nature of this shot is startling—and by virtue of its extreme departure in style must be motivated in Ford's aesthetic by an equally powerful change in content. This shot emphasizes the Joads' isolation from the misery of the camp inhabitants. The blank, indifferent gazes of these people and the mechanical movement of the Joads' truck through them gives the impression of the Joads' seeing them as mere objects to be passed through. The subjective camera dehumanizes both parties, the Joads and the other migrants. But it is the eyes of these people that shame the Joads into reaching out. Minutes later they share their meal with the camp children. From this point, at virtually the exact midpoint of the film, the Joads' sense of community intensifies, and, not coincidentally, the family's disintegration increases.

It is during the second half of the film that the major differences between it and the novel appear. I would contend that the primary effect of these changes is to emphasize the positive values of the Joads' growing collectivism, while mourning the breakup of their family. First, in the novel there are threats of and actual desertions within the family before or during the Hooverville camp scene, while in the film all defections occur or are discovered after this scene. Or, in the case of Noah, he simply disappears from the film. (Though his defection was cut from the final film in order to shorten its running time, its effect is to minimize any possible pre-Hooverville defections.)

As to the celebrated reversal in the film of the novel's Government Camp and Peach Ranch order, I would claim this is the screenwriter's effort to make the Joads' collectivism both more motivated and more progressive. The film's order shows the Joads confronted by greater and greater injustices and exploitation. By placing the Government Camp scene *after* their experiences in the Hooverville camp and the Peach Ranch the Joads' willingness to engage in collective action becomes understandable, and we can see the positive effects of such action. The novel's order undermines whatever good was experienced at the Government Camp. There is no question, then, that the film's structure determines a more positive effect. But I would argue that this structure was not cynically employed simply to pander to the sentimental needs of the audience (which it may partially have been), but that its real value is to demonstrate the motivation behind the Joads' very real change from familial individualism to societal collectivism. And this shift is at the heart of the film's primary theme: the demise of agrarian individualism.

Finally the other major change from the novel has to do with a dance floor. Ford, as we all know, has always charged his many dances with great emotional, thematic, and mythic significance. By placing the Government Camp scene in a penultimate position both Johnson and Ford were able to capitalize on Steinbeck's insignificant dance scene. The dance floor becomes the place where the migrant workers make their first effective use of collective, nonviolent action, and it is the place where Tom bids a final farewell to his mother. This spatial unity yokes, then, societal collectivism and family distintegration. The Joads do change, and the dance floor becomes in the film the final indexical signifier of that change. In fact, it could well have been Ford himself who devised this spatial unity, since in the screenplay Tom says good-bye to Ma in back of their tent. The screenplay also fails to have Tom dance with Ma while singing "The Red River Valley." This and the song's presence as Tom disappears across the dance floor into the darkness reinforce both Ma's connection with the soil and the song's elegiac function. It is all further proof that the myth of American agrarianism can live on only in the mythic soul of Ma, the great Earth Mother. Tom, the quest hero, disappears through Ma's point of view with the dance floor between them. We seem to see their dance together in our imaginations as "The Red River Valley" plays over a reverse angle shot of Ma stranded on the far side of the dance floor. Ma goes in search of the agrarian dream, while Tom searches for collective action that will bring justice to those dispossessed by the failure of American agrarianism.

Tobacco Road (1941)

Tobacco Road represents the death rattle of American agarianism. While *The Grapes of Wrath* offered some hope for an ideal, *Tobacco Road* only allows the Lesters a six-month reprieve before they are inevitably thrown off the land their family had farmed for generations and sent to the poor farm. *Tobacco Road* is a picture of stagnation, whereas *Grapes* was about change. Their basic patterns of mise-en-scène confirm this: *Grapes* shows continual movement from one place to another, conforming to the on-the-road and search genres; *Tobacco Road*, however, begins and ends in the same place, celebrates inertia, and shows what movement there is to be frantic, futile, and absurd. In *Tobacco Road* there is no possibility for change and no hope for an agrarian reality; only the hollow echo of the agrarian myth survives. This, for instance, is one of the last exchanges between Jeeter (Charley Grapewin) and his gaunt, long-suffering wife, Ada (Elizabeth Patterson) *after* they have received their miraculous reprieve:

> JEETER: "Goin' to be a great year for cotton."
> ADA: "When you goin' to do all these big things?"
> JEETER: "Oh, pretty soon—next week, maybe."

The mise-en-scène supports these words. The light is fading while Jeeter sits on the still-unfixed porch plank and dozes off into his slothful slumber. Jeeter will never grow anything ever again, nor will his children, who have abandoned their parents in a way that would do violence to Tom Joad's values. There is no future on Tobacco Road and nowhere to go. Caldwell's apocalyptic ending has Jeeter and Ada burned to ashes by the broom-sedge fire that prepares the land for plowing; Ford's and Johnson's apocalypse is of the entropic sort. In both versions, though, Jeeter goes out daydreaming about plowing and planting. Both films have been accused of muffling the political content of their literary sources. However, both films have accurately expressed each novel's relationship to the myth of American agrarianism, which in itself represents a powerful political reality. While *Tobacco Road* envisions the death of agrarianism, *The Grapes of Wrath* both keeps the dream alive and suggests a shift away from agrarian individualism.

That *Tobacco Road* has a bleaker vision of the agrarian possibilities can be partially explained by its southern setting. Instead of the Jeffersonian model of a democracy based upon small, individually owned and worked farms, southern agrarianism developed out of the European and Hamiltonian concepts of large plantations that were not worked by their owners. First slaves, then sharecroppers, worked the land. This broke the essential Jeffersonian bond between the democratic value of land ownership and the moral value of working one's own land. The Lesters' shiftlessness can be attributed to this rupture. In the film a prologue declares that the Lesters had once been the aristocracy of Tobacco Road. Now they are sharecroppers, poor whites, white trash. No matter on which side of this hierarchical scheme they fell, working the land offered them nothing of value. If they owned the land, they believed their station implied a moral imperative *not* to work it, and if they were sharecroppers, they were deprived of the democratic value of working their *own* land. In this way, southern agrarianism as a pragmatic reality was doomed to failure, for it existed almost entirely as a mythical, mystical attachment to the *idea* of the land. It was, in fact, not American agrarianism at all, but a blend of two anachronistic ideals, the Virgilian pastoral and the myth of the southern plantation.[8]

It is entirely appropriate, then, that Johnson should write a prologue for the film that juxtaposes the past with the present. The twelve shots that comprise the visual component of the prologue show decay and poverty, as well as a faded, elegiac beauty. The voice-over narration first calls attention to the presentness of this visual reality: "This is Tobacco Road today." Then while these images roll by, the narration describes the history of the myth:

> But a hundred years ago when the first Lesters came to Georgia it was different. Fifteen miles down the ridge to the Savannah River, past cotton and tobacco plantations of the Old South, past fine, big homes that the Lesters themselves built and live in. That was a hundred years ago. Came a time when the land fell fallow, and worse and worse. But you think that the Lesters would leave it? No sir! They stayed on and on. But all that they had and all that they were, that's all gone with the wind and the dust.

Then for symmetry, closure, and a return to the present the prologue repeats: "And this—this is Tobacco Road today." The film abruptly shifts its tone to wild comedy in the manner of boisterous, bizarre, and grotesque Old Southwest folk humor. All of this signifies that the stately myth of the southern plantation is dead—gone with the wind. The film proper then raises the question of whether that myth can be replaced by the myth and reality of American agrarianism. That is, can the Lesters become self-sufficient by working the land? The myth of the southern plantation has made it difficult for the myth of American agrarianism to survive, and impossible for its reality to exist at all.

Tobacco Road is essentially apocalyptic because the American dream has collapsed. For the Lesters, unlike the Joads, there is no new frontier, no new level of civilization, no new democratic action, and no new Adam. The only constituent part of the American dream left to them is a vestige of individualism. Jeeter's horror of the poor farm is that it will strip him of that, too. This fear is confirmed when he learns that the poor farm residents must wash before supper. Individualism is expressed in *Tobacco Road* solely through absurd and obsessive comic behavior. This grotesque brand of comedy has contributed to both the novel's and the film's lack of critical acceptance. However, if their tasteless, broad humor is placed within the context of Northrop Frye's theory of the phases of comedy as well as of Old Southwest folk humor, its intent and effect become quite clear. Old Southwest humor is pe-

culiarly American, characterized by indiscriminate violence, animalis-
tic behavior, debased sexuality, and grotesque physical deformities.[9]
From this folk perspective one can then see the mythical dimension of
Caldwell's most bizarre creation: "Ragged, forlorn, but irresistably
comic, Jeeter Lester is like some fabled beast-man out of folklore or
backwoods legend."[10] It is *Tobacco Road's* connection to myth, its
apocalyptic vision, and its elegiac association with romance that qualify
it as an example of Frye's sixth phase of comedy, which presents "the
collapse and disintegration of the comic society."[11] Within the framework of the Southern Gothic tradition *Tobacco Road* comedy celebrates the buffoons and parasites of a decaying world. The tobacco
roaders act out their St. Vitus' Dance within the confines of their small,
closed, and idle world.

The similarities and distinctions between these films make their interaction most instructive. In Frye's theory of mythos comedy and
romance represent different myths. Still, the mythic cycle is evolu-
tionary. Thus, the sixth phase of comedy, the apocalyptic phase, is the
one that precedes romance; according to this juxtaposition apocalyptic
comedy and wish-fulfilling romance are closely related. And since the
collapse is followed by the dream, we could argue by analogy that the
comic realism of *Tobacco Road* precludes any hope of achieving the
American dream while the romance of *The Grapes of Wrath*, on the
other hand, allows the dream to live.

And, as we have already seen, *The Grapes of Wrath* is a dream film.
Tom Joad and Jim Casy, then, are the dream saviors who follow upon
Tobacco Road's ruination. *The Grapes of Wrath* has replaced *Tobacco
Road's* southern hopelessness with western hope, stagnation with
movement, grotesque dehumanization with dignified humanization,
comic individualism with the earnest search for community, worthless
offspring with generational continuity, and handout survival with self-
sufficiency. The comedy and stagnation of *Tobacco Road* stand apart
from the romance and movement of *The Grapes of Wrath*. The prologue establishes *Tobacco Road's* pattern of visual stasis: stationary
camera, confined settings, and an absence of movement, punctuated
periodically by wild and senseless behavior. The framing and mise-en-
scène have a snapshotlike quality, while the editing reinforces the
stasis with its numbing uniformity. This film is shot and edited as
though one almost-still photograph after another were put on a reel.
The emphasis is on one-shots that emphasize the breakup of the family
and the increasing isolation, even, of Jeeter from Ada. Even their
movements intensify this sense of stagnation: Ada continually rocks in
her rocking chair, Jeeter languishes on the porch steps, and their son
endlessly throws a ball against their shack.

Ford's understanding of mythic ritual action in his romances has been transformed into the absurd repetitive behavior of comedy. These activities, futile in themselves, are made almost legendarily so by their repetition: Jeeter's reflex action of trying to inflate a sievelike inner tube; the broken porch board that flips up every time Jeeter sits on it; the always-aborted spring planting fever that inevitably ends moments after it has begun with Jeeter sitting on that porch board attempting to inflate that inner tube; and Jeeter's incessant plan to haul to town wood that no one will ever buy. Finally, there are Sister Bessie's (Marjorie Rambeau) useless attempts at religious conversions through song. While the surface function of these actions is comedic, they veer toward myth in a negative manner. They are hollow, ritual actions that by their very inefficacy demonstrate the failure of the agrarian myth. Songs that should inspire a sense of community, don't; inner tubes that should contribute to a smooth-running farm, don't; porch boards that should indicate a solid agrarian home, don't. The only movement with direction is that toward dissolution. By the end of the film all the Lester children have left. The summer morning light of the film's beginning has become the autumn twilight of its ending.

The novel's setting is so confined that it inevitably became a stage play. Johnson and Ford opened up the spatial confines of their predecessors without disturbing their disquieting stagnation. The film's creators built in a leave-and-return structure by inventing a device for Jeeter's movements: Jeeter, in the film alone, schemes to find enough money to stay on the land. This both motivates and frees his actions. It allowed the Hollywood dream moguls to believe that Jeeter tried, at least. He has been humanized by his comic inventiveness and his struggle, however futile.

Though *Tobacco Road* and *The Grapes of Wrath* are separated by their place in the progression of the myth of American agrarianism, they are bound together by their common concern for that myth. Caldwell's politically conscious novels at least partially paved the way for Steinbeck's mammoth romance about Okies. Sylvia Jenkins Cook in her book on southern poor whites in America fiction criticizes Steinbeck's novel in the same terms that many have criticized the filmed adaptation of that novel:

Steinbeck avoids any political programs in a situation fraught with partisan sympathies and concentrates instead on a vaguer philosophical resolution. The resulting ideology, a kind of transcendental agrarianism, seems feasible only in a preindustrial utopia, and for this the plot takes a suitably nostalgic course. By setting the poor white finally in motion, no matter how involuntarily, on the pioneer trail to the Pacific, Steinbeck could explore the relevance of seemingly outmoded nineteenth-century ideals to the current situation and at the same time cast off some of the more antiheroic vestiges of the poor white's literary tradition."[12]

This explains why Steinbeck's novel was more popular than Caldwell's (though the Broadway version of *Tobacco Road* had an extraordinarily long run) and why the film of Steinbeck's novel was more popular than the film of Caldwell's: the Steinbeck version of agrarianism played to the American dream, whereas the Caldwell version didn't. But the films, apart from this major distinction, have much in common, and the Zanuck-Johnson-Ford team capitalized on their similarities. Zanuck must have hoped that the success of *Grapes*, the smash hit that *Tobacco Road* had become on Broadway, and the Johnson-Ford partnership would insure a blockbusting financial return on *Tobacco Road*. Try though they did to make *Tobacco Road* a successful sequel to *The Grapes of Wrath*, America's love affair with the American dream and the agrarian ideal doomed that film's appeal to mass culture.

Still, the similarities between the two films are striking. Both screenplays mute any pointed political attack in favor of a generalized "Machine in the Garden" approach. Both films have scenes in which the men who must give the tenant farmers their notice arrive in shiny new automobiles and stay in them. Then they refuse to acknowledge responsibility for their actions. These representatives of civilization in both films say basically what the one in *Tobacco Road* does: "It's not my land and not my bank, and I just haven't got any choice." And, just as Muley tried to claim his moral ownership of the land, Jeeter Lester acknowledges the same principle, but relinquishes his claim: "Now I don't own it, an' you don't own it, an' the darn banks own it, an' they never had nothin' to do with it." And, finally, there are the almost identical shots of the Joads' and Lesters' empty shacks left with doors flapping and leaves swirling after they have been abandoned. The land is barren in both shots. What distinguishes these two films from each other as occupying different places in the progression of the myth of American agrarianism is that the Joads never return to the desolation, whereas the Lesters do.

4

The Myth of American Individualism: The Cavalry Trilogy

IN THE SEVEN FILMS Ford made from 1939 through 1941 his two preoccupations had been the effects of economic deprivation on the family and society and the dangerous challenges facing frontier democracies. Ford showed that cycles of disintegration were taking place. If these seven films were taken as a whole, disregarding the chronology of either their making or their strict historical setting, this progression would emerge: (1) In *How Green Was My Valley* economic exploitation destroys the close but paternalistic Old World Morgan family, scattering the sons out onto the frontiers of the New World. (2) In *Drums along the Mohawk* Gil Martin becomes the first of Ford's New World frontiersmen, a yeoman. He cultivates the land, begins a family, fights for American independence, and lives to see the beginning of a democracy. (3) Young Abe Lincoln endures a personal tragedy in a later and still more western frontier. He struggles to transcend that tragedy and works for the reunification and rebirth of America. (4) This allowed Ringo and Dallas in *Stagecoach* to emerge from a barren, new frontier and forge a new American community. (5) The twentieth century, however, created banks, bulldozers, and scientific cultivation to drive communities out of the Dust Bowl toward the last frontier, California, only to discover that the frontier had closed. Some, like the Lesters of *Tobacco Road*, stayed on their land and became graveyard ghosts. Others, like Tom Joad in *The Grapes of Wrath*, left to become outlaw wanderers. (6) Wanderers in search of new frontiers during World War II, became the lost, rootless merchant seamen of *The Long Voyage Home*. The tensions of individualism vis-à-vis community were always close to the surface of these films: How much individual expression would be tolerated in an Old World patriarchy? Did individualism have to be suppressed for the good of the community in an emerging democracy? Was Lincoln's powerful authority oppressive? Did economic privation strip human beings of their individual dignity? Was the outlaw the final, tragic manifestation of individualism on the closed frontier?

The American individualist: John Wayne as man-against-the-sky in Rio Grande. *Courtesy of* Phototeque.

With these questions unresolved, John Ford went off to war. World War II might well have seemed like the last frontier. Ford was fascinated by the tensions, conflicts, and paradoxes of serving in the Navy, an authoritarian, hierarchical institution that was the product of American democracy. He fought to defend a democracy that was forced to suspend and abuse many democratic rights. After the war he directed films that placed individualists in rigidly structured institutions and cultures. It would have been too easy to scrutinize the myth of American individualism within the context of a free and open civilian society. Instead, for the next thirteen years Ford explored these tensions in military situations: A Navy PT Boat Squadron in the Philippines just after Pearl Harbor, *They Were Expendable*; the Seventh Cavalry in the West after the Civil War, "the Cavalry trilogy"; a loyal West Pointer left behind to hold the fort during both world wars, *The Long Gray Line*; a naval officer dying to find combat in World War II, *Mr. Roberts*; and the true story of Spig Wead, a Navy flyer and crippled writer, *The Wings of Eagles*.

It has often been observed that the history of Western civilization has been structured on the interplay and ever-changing equilibrium between organization and individualism.[1] However, the balance shifted toward individualism with the founding of the New World. After all, it was in response to the religious, governmental, and economic strictures of Europe that bands of dissidents, adventurers, disadvantaged, and foolhardy rebels came to America. But once in America, many pioneers reestablished strict laws and codes of behavior through their religious sects and Puritan theocracy. Once again, those who most valued individualism moved west. Each successive frontier contained society's most hardened individualists. But the frontier was also defined by the organized communities that sprang up on the heels of the hardiest pioneers. So there was always a blending of wilderness individualists, frontier individualists, and civilized individualists, and each became progressively more willing to organize.

The myth of American individualism grew within the hothouse of free land, economic opportunity, social equality, self-reliance, lack of tradition, lawlessness, and pragmatism. The frontier meant a rebirth for most pioneers. They would get away from smothering relatives, industrial poverty, governmental intrusions, and the law. They could find solitude, be at one with nature, and make their own way in the world. The nineteenth-century romantic spirit simply fed the fires of frontier individualism. While frontiersmen and women were probably not reading Emerson and Thoreau, there is no question that these men's writings both reflected the times and influenced them. Emerson in his essay, "Self-Reliance," said that, "It is only as a man puts off all foreign support and stands alone that I see him to be strong and to prevail."[2] And Thoreau in a landmark essay, "Civil Disobedience," fervently expressed the frontiersmen's general lack of respect for the law: "Law never made men a whit more just";[3] and their hatred of governmental meddling: "I heartily accept the motto, 'That government is best which governs least.'"[4] Frontier democracy encouraged individualism, while frontier isolation exaggerated it. Rugged individualism became the heroic archetype; eccentric individualism became the folk archetype. The myth was strong and loudly proclaimed, but, of course, organization was also essential to the frontier. This tension, fueled by the power of myth, was one of the great structural conflicts of the frontier. As the frontier closed and population exploded, the battle cry of freedom for the individual became both more desperate and more tenuous.

For John Ford this tension found its best model on the frontier in military units stationed far from the watchful eyes and grasping hands of the tradition-bound institutions of West Point and Washington, D.C., for instance. Ford had spent years showing that the difficulties involved in establishing proper codes, rules, and laws for a democratic society on the frontier were awesome enough, but to establish them in a frontier military unit was staggering.

Ford himself had encountered many of these problems as head of the Navy Field Photographic Branch during World War II. His ambivalent attitudes toward the military were legendary, and they paved the way for his postwar sensibilities: (1) "Those who worked for Ford loved him for breaking every rule, just as most regular military brass hated him for the same reason," yet he strongly believed in the need for a strong chain of command. (2) Ford constantly subverted the authority of Navy brass, but retained absolute authority over his own men. (3) He was furious at the "navy's failure to guard against the initial disaster at Pearl Harbor, despite his warnings," yet he remained a loyal defender of the Navy. (4) "He fell in love with the baseball cap the U.S. Navy wears," wearing it and other sloppily idiosyncratic Navy gear, yet he would appear in impeccable full-dress uniform whenever he felt it would do him some good. (5) "He publicly despised yet secretly revered his decorations."[5] (6) He wanted to make realistic films about the war, but was also a willing propagandist.

After the war Ford's films were concerned with middle-ranking officers, as Ford himself had been, who must mediate the conflicts between subordinates and superiors. The best combat officers were individualists whose self-confident resourcefulness and care for the enlisted man were the source of their authority. These leaders have a distance and solitude that are unmistakable, yet they also have an easy camaraderie with their men. The responsibilities of command deepen their loneliness.

John Wayne is Ford's central figure in the myth of American individualism. In their four military films from 1945 to 1950 there is a clear progression in Wayne's rank and age. While the three cavalry films have become known as a trilogy, *They Were Expendable* fits so neatly into the cavalry scheme that it acts as the trilogy's prologue. In that film Wayne begins as an angry, impatient, and frustrated junior officer. In *Fort Apache* he is a wiser head being groomed for command. And though he bears the same rank in *She Wore a Yellow Ribbon*, it carries more responsibility and he wears it with greater maturity. Finally, in *Río Grande* he is the demanding but compassionate commander of Fort Starke.

After the war and particularly after Ford saw Wayne's rich performance in Howard Hawks's *Red River* (1948), Wayne became Ford's mythic American individualist. By this time Wayne's forty-one years expressed mature grace and emotion. Though he had starred in many films before 1948 and though it has always been assumed that *Stagecoach* marked the beginning of his career, it was *Red River* and *She Wore a Yellow Ribbon* that established Wayne as an actor and launched his legendary persona. Above the powerful bulk were the bewildered eyes, the quizzically wrinkled forehead, and the boyish smile of a slightly lonely, vulnerable kid who needed mothering. But there was also the laconic patience and the blustering fury, the warm authority and the absolute bullheadedness. He exuded sincerity, blunt honesty, self-reliance, innocence, and professionalism. He became not only John Ford's mythic individualist but also, in the absence of any real-life legends, America's. Wayne was the perfect counterforce to the cool bureaucrat and indecisive brass who hid behind a labyrinth of paper. Wayne was able to be outraged at his superiors without being insubordinate, and angry at his subordinates without being autocratic. The role and place of the traditional civilian hero who had stood slightly outside and above his community have been redefined in the military films. The military unit in Ford's films becomes humanized, thus forcing the hero-individualist to negotiate with it.

Fort Apache (1948)

Fort Apache, the first film of Ford's "cavalry trilogy," presents a complex and divisive situation. In it Ford was drawing on his World War II experiences and to that extent *Fort Apache* bears a close resemblance to *They Were Expendable*. Together they represent a benchmark against which the harmony of the individual and the community would be measured: both films occur on frontiers, far from the institutional command centers; both portray relationships between a commander and a younger second-in-command; both treat legendarily tragic events in American military history; and both depict situations that could easily lead to breakdowns in the essential structures of the community.

In *They Were Expendable* Ford had been too involved in the war effort to scrutinize coldly the causes of the Philippine debacle. The attack on Pearl Harbor had made America's military presence in the Philippines untenable. Few in the military were as outspoken as Ford in stating that the damage done at Pearl Harbor was unnecessary. He supervised the suppressed documentary, *December 7th*, detailing the ill-preparedness of U. S. forces. But feature films are about human tragedies. So *They Were Expendable* is about the cohesive force of individuals facing death and defeat and the price that is extracted when they sacrifice their individualism to the larger cause.

Ford's technique in his military films is to mythologize the military unit by valorizing the actions of the ordinary soldiers as they sacrifice themselves for the common good and to raise officers into the pantheon only after they have died or retired—and then only to promote the legend of the unit. The hero has changed. He has become a hero by subordinating himself, but his heroism is made possible by his also being himself. The tension and conflict that this creates is excruciating—but myths are born of conflict. Thus, the most heroic individual is the one least likely to be mythologized, and, inversely, the least heroic will be mythologized in order to contribute to the one myth that counts, the myth of the unit. In *Fort Apache* Ford tackled the myths of General George Custer, Custer's last stand, and the Seventh Cavalry. In the process, the mythic veils of Custer and his last stand were stripped away, thereby enhancing the myth of the Seventh Cavalry. Men come and go, but the tradition and function of the community remain. Still, these communities are made up of individuals—how can they live and express themselves?

Peter Bogdanovich asked Ford two essential questions about *Fort Apache*: (1) "In *Fort Apache*, do you feel the men were right in obeying Fonda even though it was obvious he was wrong and they were killed because of his error?" and (2) "The end of *Fort Apache* anticipates the newspaper editor's line in *Liberty Valance*, 'When the legend becomes a fact, print the legend.' Do you agree with that?" Ford's answers to both questions were unequivocal—Yes! His response to the first question was: Fonda "was the Colonel, and what he says goes, whether they agree with it or not."[6] Here Ford reiterates what his military films have shown us, that chain of command is the crucial structure in an organization designed to protect its citizens. In *Fort Apache* Ford confronts the extreme and tragically absurd example of this principle in order to test its strength and resiliency. Chain of command is the supreme lesson of military cohesion. What Ford goes on to say about obeying the colonel demonstrates the tragic viability of military principles as eternal metaphors: "In Viet Nam today, probably a lot of guys don't agree with their leader, but they still go ahead and do the job."[7] Ford said this in 1966, before most people understood the direction and causes of the Viet Nam War. Hindsight enables us to see that the military breakdowns in Viet Nam reflected those of society. Ford could depict unity in *They Were Expendable*, even in the midst of chaos, because it mirrored the society's cohesiveness. In *Fort Apache*, however, he seemed to be instructing more than describing. It is as though Ford, faced with the fragmentation of post-World War II society, felt he must reinstill that pride in community cohesiveness through the example of Custer's last stand.

This point of view comes into clearer focus when Ford explains his answer to the second question. It was important to print the legend "because I think it's good for the country. We've had a lot of people who were supposed to be great heroes, and you know damn well they weren't. But it's good for the country to have heroes to look up to. Like Custer—a great hero. Well, he wasn't. Not that he was a stupid man— but he did a stupid job that day. . . . On the other hand, of course, the legend has always had some foundation."[8] But what legend is Ford printing? He has exposed Custer (Colonel Owen Thursday, played by Henry Fonda) and his last stand to the kleig lights of reality. The legend he has preserved is that of the Seventh Cavalry, of the dog-faced soldier in dirty shirt blue, the common men who form the fabric of a community by observing its laws, rules, and codes. Captain Kirby York (John Wayne), Thursday's second-in-command, is one of these men.

Though Colonel Thursday represents virtually every negative quality imaginable, still Ford shows him to be a valuable figure because he acted honorably and died gallantly in an event that had legendary ingredients. Since legends are "good for the country," it is the responsibility of a society to exploit certain facts and suppress others in the quest to create myths. Mythologizing these kinds of events and people is less possible in today's world of instant and total systems of communication. Too much is revealed, whereas the world of myths requires that much remain concealed. *Fort Apache* is the anatomy of a myth, and as such it exposes how human beings and truths must be sacrificed so that myths may live. The tragic ironies that this mythic vision fostered were not lost in Ford's films. The least deserving of men, Colonel Thursday, became the standard bearer of a lengendary event. Even in the film industry, myths were what they had always been, tales based on skeletal facts embellished by artists and popularizers that struck certain responsive chords in a society. At the time of Custer's last stand America was in the throes of a national rebirth. The Indians stood in the way of that American dream. The cavalry had been a generally despised group of outcasts doing a dirty and unappreciated job on a dust-choked frontier. There was no real societal consensus to wipe out the Indian. A mythic event was needed. Custer's last stand, like Pearl Harbor, became the catalyst that bonded this country's resolve, for better or for worse.

What makes *Fort Apache* such a complex film are its many points of view, its ironies, its paradoxical characterizations, and Ford's own ambivalences. The conflicts in this film are many: Thursday versus virtually every positive character and attitude at Fort Apache; the white man versus the Indian; the officers versus the Indian agent; regulations versus pragmatism; West Point versus the frontier; and, of course, individualism versus community. Ford's technique allowed the audience to share in and begin to understand these many contradictory points of view.

One of the best and most-overlooked examples of Ford's method can be shown in Thursday's relationship with his daughter, Philadelphia (Shirley Temple), and his attitude toward her romance with a young lieutenant, Michael O'Rourke (John Agar). Since the death of his wife Thursday had become overprotective of and dependent on Philadelphia—an understandable reaction. But his condescending elitism toward O'Rourke and his family is unacceptable behavior. Thursday's concern for his daughter's safety is natural, so his anger at O'Rourke for taking her on a dangerous ride is justified, except that he overreacts. His love for his daughter is what humanizes him, even as it angers us. Philadelphia is a coy, dopey girl (one of the major criticisms leveled against this film is Shirley Temple's acting), yet her love for a serious and positive character like O'Rourke, her devotion to her father, and the obvious affection the rest of the fort feels for her force us to reevaluate our reactions (whether Ford intended this or not is difficult to determine).

While the myth of Custer's last stand was created to make the white man revile the Indian, still, time and the facts have redressed the balance. Nevertheless, when the Apache thunder toward Thursday's men, the audience's reaction must be horrifyingly ambivalent. If there is pleasure in knowing that Thursday will get what he deserves, there is also the tragic realization that Collingwood's (George O'Brien) transfer has just come through and that Sergeant Major O'Rourke (Ward Bond) will never live to see his grandchildren. By the same token, Cochise is shown to be an honorable leader who wishes peace. When the dust settles, the Indians have been justifiably avenged, the men of the cavalry tragically sacrificed, and Colonel Thursday partially redeemed.

Two great leaders, York and Cochise, the ones forgotten by the myth, confront each other once more. York, at the mercy of Cochise, drops his weapons and disappears into the cloud of dust to face the destroyers of Custer. When their shrouded meeting is over, the dust settles, leaving York standing alone next to Thursday's guidon which was driven into the battleground by Cochise as a final act of defiance and peace. It is also a symbol of the sacrifices endured and mediation achieved. Thursday and his men were the price paid for mediation. It is one of Ford's privileged moments because it is such a crystalline expression of reality and myth, and because it was forgotten by the myth.

Instead, what is remembered is filled with irony: the final scene of the film in which York addresses the press in front of the heroic portrait of Thursday. One of the reporters looks at the portrait and talks about how this will bring "more glory" to the regiment. York enters the frame (we have been allowed to take in the irony of the portrait and the final battle for a moment). What is so immediately striking about York is his stiff, well-pressed, carefully coiffed resemblance to Thursday. As he centers himself in the frame, he symbolically blocks out the image of Thursday. But then he moves slightly to the side so that Thursday remains in the background, looking over York's shoulder. The visual signifiers of dress, placement, and movement convey continuity. Then, with unqualified awe the reporter says that Thursday "must have been a great man—and a great soldier." York's response is a brilliant mixture of inner control, bitterness, irony, and truth: "No man died more gallantly—nor won more honor for his regiment." What would be served, he must be asking himself (and so is Ford), by attempting to set the record straight? But it has been set straight for the audience, Ford's real constituents.

York's role as a positive leader is to mediate and negotiate the truths of myth and reality. So, significantly, York will not allow one particular fact to remain clouded. The reporter asks, "What of Collingworth?" York, with little restraint, bitterly corrects him, "Colling*wood*." Then he turns to the window to give his speech (probably listened to halfheartedly by the reporters, offscreen) about how the regulars will never die so long as the cavalry lives. These men, reflected in the window and superimposed on York, ride across the American frontier, through the heart of York, and into the minds of the audience. To York, the legend of Thursday's charge can help keep those men alive. That is what matters. The reporter, with little feeling but good intentions, says, "That's the ironic part of it. We always remember the Thursdays, but the others are forgotten." Ford has made this film for "the others."

But what of Thursday? At the end of his soliloquy York says of the regiment, "They're better men than they used to be. Thursday did that. He made it a command to be proud of." And as though to reinforce these words, to show that they are not hollow platitudes, York

*York (John Wayne) contributing to the myth of Thursday/Custer (Henry Fonda)
shown in the portrait in* Fort Apache. *Courtesy of* Phototeque.

takes the reporters out to meet Thursday's family and grandson, Michael Thursday York O'Rourke. York and Thursday have been yoked by the name of Thursday's grandson and York's godson. Then York leaves, putting on Thursday's most distinctive article of dress, the desert cap. In resurrecting Thursday in this way Ford took his boldest step, opening the way to charges of false piety, charlatan mythmaking, and sentimentality.

What makes Thursday so difficult to comprehend is that he embodies the extremes of both individualism and community. In adhering rigidly and stubbornly to his own ideas he earns York's, Ford's and (perhaps) our own grudging respect, as well as contempt. Thursday exhibits his embrace of community values through decorum, dress, tradition, and chain of command. Yet on the basis of personal whim he violates those same cherished rules. He shows his displeasure at having to dance with the Sergeant Major's wife; he barges into the O'-Rourke home uninvited to dress down Michael. At Thursday's first meeting with his officers he demotes Collingwood on the basis of personal enmity. He adheres to the established models of West Point and European battles, thereby disrupting the newer but more appropriate traditions of frontier fighting. He demands that dress code be West Point regulation, but wears his own desert-style hat. He is a figure so at odds with himself that there are suggestions he is mentally unbalanced. In his first speech to the officers his train of thought swings so wildly between defining the exact nature of army regulations and justifying his own actions in such personal terms that he seems to come unhinged. Throughout the film he is vain, cold, fastidious, inflexible, arrogant, petty, vengeful, elitist, and racist; he is interested in winning glory for himself; he is a martinet; and he refuses to acknowledge any point of view other than his own. How then can he possibly redeem himself? Ford never attempts to whitewash this litany against him. Instead, his partial redemption rests on these essential elements: Ford's desire to let the dead rest in peace; that Thursday commanded in a position of command; that he accepted full responsibility for his actions; that he returned to the battle to die with his men; and that his death is useful to the myth of the Seventh Cavalry.

York watched and learned from Thursday, both the good and the bad. He will be a better leader for it. The continuity and improvement of an important community are more important to Ford than the glorification of a disastrous leader. Ford took the long view. Perhaps this is why he was able to develop so patiently the John Wayne persona into his model leader. This figure was flexible, pragmatic, and humane; he attempted to keep the peace, but fought honorably and hard when forced to; he repected the values, traditions, and points of view of his enemy; he knew the lore and nuances of his environment; he shared an easy camaraderie with his men, while he also retained their respect; he relied on the importance of chain of command, but believed that certain circumstances demanded its circumvention; he understood the need for both consensus and authority; he took full and complete authority for all his actions and for those subordinate to him; he found the middle ground between individualism and community. This was Ford's consummate military professional, individual hero, and mythic mediator.

She Wore a Yellow Ribbon (1949)

By 1949 Wayne was capable of playing the grizzled, graying, beloved Captain Nathan Brittles, who makes "young lieutenants jump when I growl." Though *She Wore a Yellow Ribbon* is the second film of the cavalry trilogy, it is very different from *Fort Apache* in tone, method, and structure. It was also the trilogy's only color film. Ford had always preferred working in black and white, particularly for dramatic stories, believing that "black and white is real photography."[9] When Ford worked in color he took the same care and control over nuances of composition, shading, and lighting that he had with black-and-white film. Ford used color with films he considered to be more episodic than dramatic. He rarely distorted color for dramatic purposes. Instead, he allowed the natural beauty of carefully selected, framed, and composed locations to shine through. In *She Wore a Yellow Ribbon*, though, Ford added some artifice: "I tried to copy the [Frederic] Remington [the great turn-of-the-century painter of the American West] style there—you can't copy him one hundred percent—but at least I tried to get in his colour and movement, and I think I succeeded partly."[10] The Remington style and the episodic story shot in color signify unity and harmony, rather than the harsher dialectical tensions of *Fort Apache* or *Río Grande*. It is a graceful and poignant tribute to a beloved leader wrapped in the myth of the integrated individualist.

Captain Nathan Brittles is Ford's great leader, yet he has only limited command. Major Allshard (George O'Brien, promoted to his rightful place in this film after the ignominy of *Fort Apache*) is in command of the fort. Captain Brittles leads a troop. In this film there is absolutely no friction between the two leaders. Brittles may be outraged at having to take two women out on patrol, but his formal protest to Major Allshard is both good-natured and serious. While he knows an order is an order, he still files a useless formal protest. Allshard even helps Brittles with his spelling. Brittles will take women with no rancor. Brittles and Allshard fit hand-in-glove. Ford refuses to allow the responsible individual to overpower the restrictions of his community, and yet with each succeeding film of the trilogy he endows his hero with greater individualism.

In *She Wore a Yellow Ribbon* Wayne's character has been given a wider berth. The commanding officer fades into the background. The real frontier is not in a fort, but out on patrol. There Brittles makes his own decisions, creates his own plans, and shoulders full responsibility. At the fort he is constantly reminded of his limitations: the orders from his superior, the rigid rules of retirement, the passing on of a command. Though he chafes at these controls, he always accepts them. All the tensions of this film emanate from this conflict between individual freedom and community restriction, but they are always resolved because harmony is this film's subject and because none of the tensions is as fundamentally dangerous as those between Thursday and York in *Fort Apache*.

This film is concerned with the problem of how communities retire their quintessential leaders. Will the cavalry simply cut Nathan Brittles loose to drift alone into the sunset? We don't want them to and Ford can't bring himself to permit it. This tells us a great deal about Ford and individualism. While there is no question that Brittles is an unforgettable character, full of warmth, gruffness, and private sadness, he achieves the fruits of his individualism through his interaction with the community. Ford's military films demonstrate that individuals cannot exist without a community, nor can a community survive without individuals. So Captain Brittles is brought back into the community he so loves, and is promoted. Why? Because he can still be of use to the cavalry and because communities should shelter their own. That is where the Brittleses of the world belong because that is where they are best able to express their individualism. This framework allowed Ford to demonstrate the unique mediating power of the frontier's myth of American individualism. The wilderness had allowed unfettered individual freedom, while civilization demanded the repression of individualism. The frontier, however, afforded a tense interplay and balance between the two.

Nathan Brittles and his men are drenched in the dream world of memory. The film's rationale is found in the retirement inscription the men compose for Brittles, "Lest We Forget." This was also the rationale for *They Were Expendable* and *Fort Apache*, which had been eulogies to swabbies and dog-faced soldiers.

She Wore a Yellow Ribbon opens on the memory of Custer's last stand. It is a perfect transition into the second film of the trilogy. The voice-over narration announces the event and cloaks it in mythic language: "Custer is dead. And around the bloody guidon of the immortal Seventh Cavalry lie two hundred and twelve officers and men." That guidon is, figuratively, the same one that Cochise drove into the ground at Kirby York's feet in *Fort Apache*. The dead are those lying in the dust and riding through York's mind at the end of that film. Now Brittles and Allshard (who are, really, reincarnations of York and Collingwood) remember some of their old friends as the sunset outside the window turns bloodred, the red of nightmare. (In 1956 Ford would repeat this same stylized lighting to foreshadow the massacre of Ethan Edwards's family in *The Searchers*.) At the conclusion of *She Wore a Yellow Ribbon* the leader has achieved a greater stature and the cavalry a more established place in the growth of a nation than either had by the end of *Fort Apache*. In the tragic *Fort Apache* they were eulogized whereas in the episodic *Yellow Ribbon* they are memorialized: "So here they are, the dog-faced soldiers, the regulars, the fifty-cents-a-day professionals, riding the outposts of the nation. From Fort Reno to Fort Apache, from Sheridan to Starke, they were all the same—men in dirty shirt blue, and only a cold page in the history books to mark their passing. But wherever they rode, and whatever they fought for, that place became the United States." Ford's harmonious, celebratory, autumnal color film is meant to flesh out the individualism that has been lost in the "cold page in the history books."

In *She Wore a Yellow Ribbon* we get closer to the life and rituals of the leader and the cavalry. Since this is a film of integration, we are shown both the private rituals of Nathan Brittles, those that enhance his individualism, and the public rituals of the cavalry, those that confirm the codes of the community. The early morning wake-up call and the evening report to his dead wife are the private rituals that form his public cavalry life. In the first, Sergeant Quincannon (Victor Mc-Laglen) enters each morning to find Brittles in his red BVDs. We are privy to Brittles's quarters, where we find him out of military dress. This private glimpse also establishes Brittles's close, bantering friend-ship with Quincannon, his comic noncom alter ego. With Quincannon, Brittles can break cavalry rules by allowing Quincannon to hide a bot-tle in his vase, can display the remnants of a small but precious per-sonal life, can share a few private moments before his public life begins each day, and can first voice his personal credo, "Never apologize, it's a sign of weakness." This morning ritual is comic and life-affirming. The evening ritual, the quietly legendary "Brittles report," to his late wife is lonely and elegiac. Both, however, turn on the living presence of memory. Brittles takes a watering can to keep the flowers at the gravestone alive, just as he takes a stool to sit and keep the memory of his wife alive. In between these private rituals of morning and evening the rituals of cavalry life are played out: the readying of C Troop, the coffee with Allshard, the retirement ceremony, the various duties of command, the dance, the barroom fight, the powwow with Pony That Walks, and the burial of Trooper Smith. Captain Nathan Brittles is a proud, strong, self-reliant, and lonely man; he is also a man lost with-out the social and structural fabric of his community, the cavalry.

This intermingling of the private and public creates a number of contradictory responses in Brittles. While he loves to see young lieu-tenants jump, he can barely contain his sniffles when he reads the inscription on the watch. While he says that it's a sign of weakness to apologize, he finds himself tacitly apologizing—with Ford's blessing. Though he returns to the cavalry during a dance in his honor, he leaves it to give his report to his wife. Though he is a northerner, he allows a Confederate burial, and though he is a white man, he respects the Indians. But these seemingly inconsistent reactions only confirm Brit-tles's role as Ford's most integrated individualist and mediator. His private rituals both express his individuality and mingle his personality with the timeless rituals of the cavalry. "The army," says Brittles, "is always the same. The sun and the moon may change, but the army knows no seasons." It is mythical.

On an aesthetic level *She Wore a Yellow Ribbon* marked a decidedly new direction for Ford. *My Darling Clementine* was the first of Ford's postwar films to drop the determinedly dramatic visual, narrative, and thematic structures that had characterized the bulk of his great prewar films. But with *She Wore a Yellow Ribbon* the so-called "late Ford" style moved into full swing. Ford's decision to shoot in color indicated a move away from dramatically constructed films. This more episodic style emphasized characterization over thematic confrontation, natural environment over studio setting, private rituals over public ones, flow of images over unified scenes, and subtly functional camera work over dramatic setups. *She Wore a Yellow Ribbon* is, with the exception of the unimportant *Gideon of Scotland Yard*, the most episodic, linear, and non-narratively plotted film Ford ever made. It was an effort to bring greater realism to his filmmaking. Ironically, this change coincided with America's critical and commercial infatuation with a very different style of realism, one that depicted grim, naturalistic, black-and-white dramas of urban entrapment or social muckraking. Many of those films—*All the King's Men, Death of a Salesman, From Here to Eternity, On the Waterfront, Marty, Come Back Little Sheba*, and others—today seem dated and inordinately contrived. Only the "B" *noir* pictures—virtually ignored in their own day—seem realistically alive with timelessly sleazy angst.

Ford's realism was usually misunderstood and dismissed as an old man's distinterest in dramatic conflict, a crochety adherence to old values, and a legend's laziness concerning visual heightening. Color films became the unimaginative norm, so for socially radical filmmakers a return to black and white signified a return to realism. But Ford realized that black and white was a stylization in itself and that color, if carefully implemented, could represent the new realism. Even further, if exaggerated deliberately and judiciously, color could also suggest alternate states of reality—dreams and nightmares, for instance. Ford also wanted his films to express more directly the common rhythms, textures, and details of the hero's and his community's whole life. But, and this is the essential "but" of his career, he was not about to sacrifice the reality of myth.

For Ford, the reality of cavalry life was movement through the vast, empty, beautiful but dangerous frontier of the Southwest. Ford's films became tone poems on the feel and shape of private events—regardless of how public they may seem. Never before had Monument Valley been so much a part of the complete environment of those who moved through it. And never had Ford so completely immersed audiences in the endless walking, riding, and bouncing through this wilderness. Almost every conceivable human emotion is played out in transit. As a result, scenes in the traditional sense have been eliminated. Dissolves rather than fades contribute to the sense of unending travel, with the bits and pieces of human relationships casually encountered along the way. One significant technique Ford developed was to begin shots with casual and mundane activities, usually without Wayne's presence. The camera then remains stationary as narrative content begins to develop. Then Wayne enters to crystallize and resolve the situation. When he leaves, the activity plays itself out, ending with either a cut or a dissolve. A transitional shot that emphasizes setting over event ends the sequence. Then the process begins all over again. Ford's takes became longer, and within these takes Ford would radically alter the composition. The casual randomness Ford gave to events broke the stranglehold that theatrical scene and sequence had held on filmmaking in the thirties and forties.

She Wore A Yellow Ribbon became a watershed film for Ford. It marked the emergence of John Wayne as a major film presence and as the heroic persona of Ford's later years. It also signaled the fruition of his postwar shift in style.

Río Grande (1950)

From the fresh-faced innocence of *They Were Expendable*, replaced by the clean-shaven frustration of *Fort Apache* and the mustachioed maturity of *She Wore a Yellow Ribbon*, the facial iconography of John Wayne's military persona turned in *Río Grande* to an unlikely figure, Colonel Owen Thursday and his fastidiously trimmed goatee in *Fort Apache*. In *Río Grande* Ford decided to explore the flip side of Colonel Thursday, and the starting place was Wayne's goatee. After *She Wore a Yellow Ribbon* Ford could take the perfectly integrated leader no further. Yet Thursday was still a burr under Ford's saddle. He was a leader who had faced tougher choices than Nathan Brittles. Could a more humane and flexible Colonel Thursday be the perfect leader? *Río Grande* answers that question.

In the beginning of *Río Grande* Kathleen Yorke (Maureen O'Hara, in the first of her series of memorable films with Wayne), Lieutenant Colonel Kirby Yorke's estranged wife, arrives unexpectedly at Fort Starke. When she first sees her husband after fifteen years, she defines him in terms that would suit Colonel Thursday: "Ramrod, wreckage, and ruin. Still the same Kirby." She in turn is characterized by Kirby as "special privilege to the special born. Still the same Kathleen." This is the film of two people mature enough to change their public personae for a last chance at savoring a private togetherness. But it is also a film about a leader who comes to realize that devotion to military duty does not necessarily exclude any expression of familial and human emotion. In fact, this emotion is what differentiates him from Thursday and makes him a greater leader.

This is the film that lays to rest the myth that individualism must oppose community. *Río Grande* takes a hard look at this issue by returning to some of the dialectical issues posed by *Fort Apache*. In that film Ford needed to express the polarities in two men; in *Río Grande* he was able to resolve them in one man. In *Fort Apache* Ford was not able to penetrate the public presence of Colonel Thursday. We never got close to Thursday's private anguish. We saw his bitterness over the command assignment, but his private thoughts on his family were missing. He remained, along with his pre-war Fordian counterparts, essentially a public figure. The black-and-white photography, the return to the York(e) character, the goatee, the exacting commander, and the presence of a wife and son are indications that Ford wished to explore further the more private dilemma of Colonel Thursday: to what extent must effective leadership and devotion to duty isolate a man from his own deeply felt human needs?

In *Río Grande* the John Wayne figure reached the highest level of command that interested Ford. As fort commander, Kirby Yorke is being pushed by his commander, General Phil Sheridan (J. Carroll Naish). Regardless of the rank achieved, chain of command must be preserved. As the consummate professional, Yorke's response is, "I'm not complaining, sir. I get paid for it." Carrying out orders is the easiest part of command, so Ford dispenses with it first. York's life becomes complicated when his son, Jeff (Claude Jarman, Jr.), who has just flunked out of West Point and whom he has never seen, appears under his command wanting to be treated just as any other private. Then Yorke's wife arrives with the intent of buying her son out of the army. The battle lines between each member of this "family" have been draw long and deep: North versus South; military versus family; "ramrod, wreckage, and ruin" versus "special privilege to the special born"; son versus father. Between the symbolic burning-down of Kirby's and Kathleen's marriage (during the Civil War, at the beginning of their marriage, Kirby had been ordered by Sheridan to burn Kathleen's ancestral plantation) and the fortuitous appearance of their son at the fort stands their long-suppressed love for each other. This is symbolized by the fragile music box that Kirby carries with him out onto the frontier. It plays "I'll Take You Home Again, Kathleen."

Río Grande has neither the hard tensions of *Fort Apache* nor the relaxed flow of *She Wore a Yellow Ribbon*. Instead, it takes the middle ground: on the one hand, working out a love story through richly evocative folk songs and the comic misunderstandings of a son's rite of passage and, on the other, confronting the formidable conflicts that stand in the way of a family's unity. *Río Grande* pits the tough rules of the military against two tough individualists who are willing to compromise for one last chance at love. Behind them lurks the ghosts of Colonel Owen Thursday with his inflexible, impersonal, and impeccable devotion to duty and authority. Kirby Yorke has become the apotheosis of the great leader because he had absorbed the qualities of Rusty Ryan (Wayne) and Brickley (Robert Montgomery) in *They Were Expendable*, Kirby York and Owen Thursday in *Fort Apache*, and Nathan Brittles in *She Wore a Yellow Ribbon*. The hardest lesson had been taught by

Thursday, who demonstrated, however unhappily, that personal isolation, cold military honor, and unswerving obedience are necessary
ingredients in a humane, effective, and individualistic military leader.
Ford demonstrates that such leadership comes only after years of pain,
loss, and sacrifice. But the result is wisdom, strength, and flexibility.
In *Río Grande* the gap between the public and the private is greater
than ever. Only exceptional courage and passion can bridge it. This
film is about that gap and that bridge.

The opening scene immediately puts Yorke's character in perspec-
tive. General Sheridan is visiting the fort and conveying orders.
Yorke's relationship with Sheridan is easy and informal; they go back a
long way together. Still, it was Sheridan who ordered Yorke to burn
Kathleen's home and who now gives him "the dirtiest job in the army."
Yorke doesn't complain; he never has and he never will. He is a professional. We see their professional and personal relationship merge when
Sheridan tells him that his son has been dismissed from West Point.
Later, while doing paperwork, Yorke hears the name of his son called
on the roll of new recruits. As he steps outside to address them, a low-
angle shot accentuates his power, as though it were a shot from the
minds of the young recruits. He paints a particularly bleak picture of
cavalry life, as though speaking to his son alone. They are first framed
together during this speech, the son in profile, foreground right, the
father in profile, middle ground left. They face each other, but on different planes, not actually making contact. In the background between
them stands the ubiquitous Quincannon (Victor McLaglen), their mediator. It is a brilliantly metonymic shot, for it contains the essentials
of their relationship.

Later, in his tent, Yorke's first words to his long-lost son are these:
"On the official record you're my son, but on this post you're just another trooper. You heard me tell the recruits what I need from them.
Twice that I will expect from you. At Chapultepec, my father, your
grandfather, shot for cowardice the son of a United States Senator. It
was his duty. I will do mine. You've chosen my way of life. I hope you
have the guts to endure it. But put out of your mind any romantic
ideas that it's a way of glory. It's a life of suffering and hardship. And
an uncompromising devotion to your oath and your duty." As with
Colonel Thursday's opening speech to his officers in *Fort Apache*, this
one reveals Yorke's confusion. The more he tries to pass himself off as
an unbending public figure, the more he lays bare his private anguish.
Thursday and Yorke are men who protest too much, though Yorke's
bluster and growl betray a softer inner man than Thursday's clinically
precise digressions did. Yorke's son does not flinch at these terms; in
fact, he accepts them wholeheartedly: "I'm not in this post to call you
'father.' I was ordered here as Trooper Jefferson Yorke of the United

State Cavalry. And that is all I wish to be, sir." Having acknowledged
that they understand each other, Yorke dismisses his son. Jeff salutes,
but does not receive a regulation salute in return. He waits until he
does. Quincannon, watching this, loves it. At this point both father
and son are hiding behind the stiff codes of military life. The cavalry
is their refuge. But the moment Jeff leaves, Kirby goes over to the spot
where Jeff was standing and measures his height against Jeff's. This
private reaching out, juxtaposed so strikingly against their public confrontation, defines the direction of this film. Kirby's finely tuned emotional control, an essential quality of any military leader, prevents him
from reaching his son on a private level. They will have to build their
relationship from the foundation of trooper and colonel. The military
that had destroyed their relationship as father and son will be one of
the instruments of its renewal.

The other factor will be the presence of the woman, the mother, the
wife, the archetypal Fordian female, Maureen O'Hara. What endeared
O'Hara to Ford was her firebrand temperament, independent spirit,
loyalty, pride, warm smile, generous eyes, and beauty. In the beginning of the film she is as cold and unbending as her husband and son.
More than any other Ford picture, this one is about the compromises
that must be made if individuals are to be united into a family, and
then only if they are further united into that larger family, the cavalry.

On the evening of Kathleen's arrival Kirby invites her to dinner in
his tent. It is a moving event. The beauty of the shadows and lines that
the kerosene lantern creates is matched only by the mature love these
two people have for each other. Of course Ford does not allow unal-
loyed romance to take over. In the most romantic shot of Kirby and
Kathleen together two dark tent poles come between them—a visual
signifier for the ever-present military divisiveness. These poles hold
up the structure that both houses and smothers Kirby and Kathleen.
At this point all military signifiers are destructive to their relationship.
Later, however, the regimental singers will serenade Kathleen with
the song, "I'll Take You Home Again, Kathleen." Though Kirby is em-
barrassed by their choice of songs and Kathleen is disappointed that it
was not Kirby's request, the family of the cavalry has taken the initia-
tive in drawing them together. Quincannon, the comic mediator,
planned this serenade.

Suddenly Kathleen goes to her son's tent. She asks him to leave with
her and return to West Point. Jeff asks her what kind of man his father
is, and she says, "He is a lonely man, a very lonely man." Jeff won't
leave because that "would be quitting." She responds, "You're stubborn and proud, Jeff, just like he is." But Jeff replies in kind, "Just like
you are, mother." There it stands. They are not a family at all, just
three lonely, proud, stubborn individuals. All struggle to maintain

York (John Wayne) and his wife, Kathleen (Maureen O'Hara), attempting a reconciliation in Rio Grande; *however, the tent pole separates them visually. Courtesy of* Phototeque.

their own private identities in the face of the seemingly rapacious cavalry. Or, as Kathleen puts it in a toast to Kirby and General Sheridan, "To my only rival, the United States Cavalry."

Ford's task was to develop the film in such a way that Kathleen would not see the cavalry as a rival, that Kirby would not devote himself to it as though it were a religious order, and that Jeff would not use it as a refuge. In this way, the cavalry could provide a structure around which the best elements of their individual personalities might grow. Each must make choices that prove to the other two that he or she is not deserting his or her identity and duty, while at the same time each is making a human commitment to the other two members of the family. Kirby, then, assigns Jeff to escort the women and the children rather than accompany the patrol: "He'll hate it, but I love you for it," Kathleen says to Kirby. By accident the children are kidnapped, allowing Jeff to prove himself in a dangerous situation. Kirby is wounded, so Jeff can pull the arrow out of his father's shoulder, thus ritualistically binding them as father and son (Kirby calls Jeff "son" for the first time as he pulls the arrow out). Kathleen, for her part, stays through the battle and becomes a waiting cavalry wife, with sleeves rolled up and white apron on. When the men return to the fort, she goes instinctively to Kirby rather than to her son.

By the end of the film the mythical and indexical configurations of Ford's world are complete. Jeff returns standing up, having endured his rite of passage; Kirby returns on a stretcher, needing help and comfort. The equation has been set right: the weaker has been strengthened and the stronger has been humbled. Kathleen has put aside her pride and has waited for them both—going to the one who needs her most. Cavalry life on the frontier is the great equalizer.

But have Kirby and Kathleen been so reduced as to have lost the energy and power that made them interesting to us in the first place? In particular, has Kathleen been relegated to the position of traditional helpmate to the male god? A surface viewing might indicate that she has, but complex issues are involved. The first is pride. Pride endows *Río Grande*, like *Fort Apache*, with its tension. Colonel Thursday is destroyed by his hubris. But *Río Grande* is the story of two people who overcome their considerable pride. The price they must pay for this, however, is Kirby's physical decline and Kathleen's wifely waiting.

As to Kathleen's role: usually the male mythic heroes of Ford's romances have been losers, widowers, or men without women. However, when the men did have women, Ford took great care to supply these women with an independent spirit. Granted, Ford's women were no Hildy Johnsons (Rosalind Russell, the wisecracking reporter of *His Girl Friday*), but his frontier settings offered fewer options. Still, it would be difficult to describe these women as shrinking violets: Jean Arthur, the reporter in *The Whole Town's Talking*; Gloria Stuart, Dr. Mudd's wife in *The Prisoner of Shark Island*; Katharine Hepburn as Mary Stuart in *Mary of Scotland*; Barbara Stanwyck, the courageous wife in *The Plough and the Stars*; Claire Treavor, the prostitute, Dallas, in *Stagecoach*; Claudette Colbert, the frontier wife in *Drums along the Mohawk*; Jane Darwell as Ma Joad in *The Grapes of Wrath*; Donna Reed, the doomed nurse in *They Were Expendable*; Joanne Dru in *She Wore a Yellow Ribbon* and *Wagon Master*; Maureen O'Hara in *The Quiet Man*, *The Long Gray Line*, and *The Wings of Eagles*; Ava Gardner as a tough, "I've been around" woman in *Mogambo*; Vera Miles in *The Searchers* and *The Man Who Shot Liberty Valance*; Linda Cristal, the Mexican woman captured by the Comanche in *Two Rode Together*; and Anne Bancroft as Dr. Cartwright in *7 Women*. All are survivors, while many are society's outcasts. When they are wives, they are often as strong, if not stronger, than their husbands. They always endure hardships in Ford's frontier settings. A few films are even shot from the woman's point of view, to give further insight into her special world: *Drums along the Mohawk* and *The Plough and the Stars*, for instance.

The women in Ford's films are neither passive appendages nor twittering helpmates. They are earthy, strong women of fire and passion.

They bring comfort and strength to their men and they fight for a piece of themselves. Often they are responsible for whatever humanity exists out on the frontier. It is true that, with the exception of 7 *Women* and *Mary of Scotland*, Ford did not make women his leading characters, but neither were they merely part of the woodwork. He may not have been in the vanguard regarding the position of women, but he presented them with affection and respect. They always maintained individual identities, even though they strove to fulfill their roles as mothers, wives, or lovers. The family was Ford's first concern, but, as film after film shows, the reality of family life rarely matched the ideal. Death, pride, poverty, restlessness, and the fragmentation of the times kept families apart. Ford's characters strove for the ideal, but always accepted the real. His women, too, struggled with the conflicts of individualism and community.

5

The Myth of American Civilization: *My Darling Clementine* and *The Man Who Shot Liberty Valance*

THE MYTH OF American civilization is the myth of America's mission and manifest destiny to expand westward into the wilderness and thereby civilize it and to do this in all righteousness. This process began almost the moment the first settlers entered the New World—which to them was a wilderness. It is the myth of American civilization because, first, the goal was to create a civilization; second, it would be peculiarly American since it would be a better and more moral civilization than the decadent ones the new settlers had left, and, third, it was a myth because it was a powerfully imaginative and ambivalent vision pitting the wilderness with its virtues and vices against those of civilization. America as a New World was empty (from a white perspective, of course) but full of resources and ripe for the cyclical process that would become known as American progress.

The first mythic cycle of progress lasted until the Civil War and generally followed this pattern: backwoodsmen entered the wilderness to escape the first sign of civilization, and though they were either unaware of or would have rejected the idea, they were the first to introduce civilizing factors into the wilderness. They paved the way for the frontiersmen. The two coexisted for a time, but the backwoodsman's need for solitude, independence, and pathfinding drove him to new wildernesses. The frontiersman, as his name and middle position implies, was the mediator between the wilderness and civilization. He oftentimes brought with him a family and attempted to eke out a living by doing some farming—two strong civilizing factors. Then came the pioneer (both male and female now), the Jeffersonian independent yeoman who came to settle down, to set roots that would be permanent, that would lead to a community. The frontiersman moved on to new frontiers because those qualities in him that were like those of the backwoodsman drove him to follow the backwoodsman. Backwoodsmen, frontiersmen, and pioneers kept following one another into the West—until, as the myth goes, the final wilderness, the post-Civil-War desert West.

American civilization invades the wilderness: the unfinished church against Monument Valley in My Darling Clementine.

95

A new configuration of the cycle was played out to take into account the beginnings of the industrial, corporate era. The first cycle envisioned civilization as a farming community. This agrarian ideal gave way to the new corporate ideal; Hamiltonianism superseded Jeffersonianism. In the first configuration all three representatives of the American civilization cycle were independent and self-sufficient. They worked for no one. But in the second configuration most of the heroes of American civilization were employees. James Oliver Robertson in *American Myth, American Reality* lists Lincoln, cowboys, Custer, and the cavalry as the post-Civil-War heroes who "bridged the gap between the old wilderness world of America and the new industrial urban world."[1] It so happens that eight of the fourteen John Ford films examined in my work take these figures as their subject. This era is central to the second cyclical configuration of American civilization because it describes, in mythic terms, the transition into America's corporate, industrial age. One can argue that in the 1930s, 40s, and 50s when American emerged as a world industrial power, these post–Civil War romances provided the country with a foundation myth for its industrial era. The heroes had to be employees because most Americans were employees, but they also had to be frontiersmen so as to keep alive the dream of freedom and independence.

Of the six films not mythically situated in this transitional post–Civil War era three are Edenic in nature. *Drums along the Mohawk*, for instance, is the only film set in the agrarian, pre-industrial era. Gil and Lana Martin represent the independent pioneer yeomen. *Judge Priest* and *Steamboat Round the Bend*, though literally post–Civil War, are figuratively Edenic. A post–Civil War Eden could exist only in the South, so this myth goes, because it was the perfect fusion of wilderness and nature in the industrial era. The North had become industrialized, hence too civilized, and the West was still too primitive. The South however, now unified with the nation, free of its moral blight, slavery, and both agrarian and cultivated, could be seen as the final Eden, the last Garden of the industrial era with Will Rogers as its Adam.

The other three films have settings contemporaneous with their making. These films depict the full force of corporate, industrial America in three different locations. *Tobacco Road* chronicles the collapse of the Southern Eden, The corporate sharecropper system had turned the garden into a weedpatch. In *Dr. Bull* Will Rogers is *the* last Adam in the completely civilized, restrictive, and bleak New England. Only out West was there hope. In *The Grapes of Wrath* the industrial era had eroded America's breadbasket, driving the tenant farmers off the land in search of some new purpose and identity. This was manifest destiny's last gasp. The myth of the frontier, an actual frontier, was still alive, though barely so, some forty-five years after the frontier had been declared officially closed.

A deepening gloom and despair seeped into the major film genres of the post-World War II era, characterized by the *noir* films of the forties and fifties, the death-of-the-west Westerns of the sixties and seventies, the deterministic world of gangsters and detectives in the seventies, the Viet Nam War films of the seventies and eighties, and the return to *noir* films in the eighties. These are all films that depict the corruption and restrictiveness of the industrial era. Are we today on the edge of a new era, the postindustrial era that may bring hope, a new cycle, the third mythical configuration? Are science fiction films the basis of a new foundation myth? Is this why the Western, as a film and television genre, no longer holds such compelling interest for mass audiences? In other words, has the foundation myth of the second cycle of American civilization, the industrial one, passed into (or is passing into) history, just as the agrarian one did? I would argue that, yes, this is happening, but that the constants of the American dream, the myths of Adam, agrarianism, frontier, democracy, and individualism, will simply be retooled to adhere to the new postindustrial cycle of American civilization. The myth of American civilization depends upon the ability of Americans to adapt and change as they seek and find new frontiers—somewhere. So while the actual heroes, settings, and tales of the post-Civil-War industrial frontier may be too remote for postindustrial audiences, the mythic characteristics of them are not. We may now study the tales as history in order to glean from them those qualities that will guide our culture into the future. I would argue that the six mythic qualities from the first two cycles of American civilization still have such a powerful grip on our actions, consciousnesses, and imaginations that they have become the undying myths of America's space frontiers (to the extent that the genre characteristics of Westerns and science fiction films have become both consciously and unconsciously similar, or, to put it crudely, space operas have replaced horse operas).

John Ford's two most explicit American-civilization films are, as they must be, about certain stages in America's dual mission to civilize the wilderness without removing the wilderness from civilization. This mythic task of mediating the irresolvable has fallen to six mythical heroes and heroines: Wyatt Earp (Henry Fonda) of *My Darling Clementine* and Tom Doniphon (John Wayne), Ransom Stoddard (James Stewart), and Hallie (Vera Miles) of *The Man Who Shot Liberty Valance* (and we should include here Ringo and Dallas of *Stagecoach*, the most wilderness-infused mediators of the earliest stage of this American civilization cycle).

In this second cycle the backwoodsman has been replaced by the frontiersman, a lone, unmarried cowboy who enters the frontier from the wilderness. This frontiersman is the soul of the frontier town, for he partially civilizes it by protecting it with his wilderness skills from wilderness forces. Four options are generally open to the frontiersman in the frontier town: he dies, moves on, is expelled, or stays. If he stays he changes into a pioneer. The pioneer of the first cycle of American civilization was an independent yeoman whose primary goal was to raise a self-sufficient family. In the second cycle the pioneer often provided services to the frontier town. Now the pioneers are no longer completely self-sufficient; they have become consumers and are willing to hire frontiersmen to protect them—so long as these frontiersmen eventually adapt to their new position as permanent members of the community. So lawmen, shopkeepers, barbers, saloon-keepers, hotel owners, and the employees of such establishments take their place beside the homesteaders as the pioneers of this second cycle.

In this second cycle the most civilized representative is the educated professional who has replaced the jack-of-all-trades pioneer. The pioneer of the first cycle simply had to survive and stay put to prove his or her worth as the most civilized representative of the cycle. The professional must prove himself, too, but in a more complicated way. His Eastern ways are more apparent; he is more clearly a representative of what the frontiersmen and pioneers were escaping. The professional is far more suspect and so must prove his frontier capabilities, which usually entail either comic or dangerous trials. These often have a double-edged conclusion: humiliation from lack of wilderness or frontier expertise and respect for the courage to try.

What makes *Clementine* and *Liberty Valance* American-civilization films is that each film depicts major transitions in the frontier's civilizing process, with the second film taking us one step further than the first. *Clementine* is a frontiersman-pioneer film, while *Liberty Valance* is a frontiersman-pioneer-professional film. Each, however, takes a critically different approach to its hero and heroes. *Clementine* is unified behind one mediator who is so capable of changing from a frontiersman to a pioneer that he alone embodies the harmony of the almost-perfect frontier state. *Liberty Valance*, as befits its more civilized state, can find no one to make its two more complex and demanding transitions. Tom Doniphon is a pioneer with the qualities of a frontiersman who could not possibly make the leap to civilized professional and Ranse Stoddard is a pioneer with professional expertise. Neither can make the frontiersman to pioneer to professional transitions. Two mediators are necessary. This difference between the two films suggests that fragmentation and specialization have become part of modern (i.e., turn-of-the-century) civilized life. It indicates the shape of things to come.

My Darling Clementine (1946)

In 1946, after World War II had affected him deeply, Ford returned to make a Western. Most Americans believed that the war had been a defense of American democracy and civilization, "the American Way of Life." *My Darling Clementine* was a celebration of America's frontier values upon its triumph (to Americans it was an *American* victory over European tyranny, decadence, and impotence). If *Stagecoach* represented America's pre-war emergence from the wilderness, then World War II quickly made it possible to see America at its zenith in the full flush of its frontier civilization. The progression of this allegory fit America's conception of itself.

One reservation remains concerning this celebration. Was too much power invested in one man, Wyatt Earp (Henry Fonda)? Ringo in *Stagecoach* was not a community leader. He might need to be later in his life with Dallas, after the close of the film, but within the film's confines he is too young, too concerned with his own problems, and too much the mediator of individual antagonisms. Wyatt is Ringo reborn into a higher stage of civilization. Wyatt's social responsibilities are greater, and with them comes the charge that he has too much power. Lincoln in Ford's 1939 film has been similarly accused, but Wyatt is a more severe case. It is known that Ford was extremely frustrated by the wartime bureaucracy. Still, in *They Were Expendable*, Ford's war film that preceded *Clementine*, he advocated teamwork over being "a one-man gang." The relationship of the individual to the community was a major preoccupation of Ford's work in the decade after the war. It was always a tension that could be mediated but not resolved. *My Darling Clementine*, made in the flush of victory, does not really deal with this issue as a problem.

Since postwar America had taken its rightful place in the world, it had to show that world that it was civilized without being decadent. So, in this allegorical Western, America is seen as a strong, vibrant, frontier culture that must retain its strength through a wilderness frontier hero, while it demonstrates its progress through a series of civilizing factors. The scheme of civilizing factors in *My Darling Clementine* is more complicated than in *Stagecoach* because there are far subtler shifts in the development of civilization. The Earps, unshaven and heading west with a herd of cattle, encounter old man Clanton (Walter Brennan) and one of his sons. Out in the wilderness where Wyatt Earp should have known better (has he become too civilized already?) he reveals—mentions in a casual, friendly way—that he and his brothers will most likely go into town for a beer and a shave. Taking advantage of this civilized exchange, the Clantons rustle the cattle and kill the remaining brother. The Earps need the amenities of civilization. Liquor is associated with frontier towns, while shaving suggests a higher civilizing factor. It is no accident, then, that the barber pole is the predominant visual signifier of the first half of the film, since Wyatt is primarily concerned with becoming civilized[2] (to the extent that his vengeance quest is put on hold during the body of the film).

When Wyatt first enters Tombstone, he heads directly for a shave at the Bon Ton Tonsorial Parlor. This establishment has all the accoutrements of dandified civilization: the name, the extra services, the "sweet smelling stuff," and the barber chair from Chicago (later in the film the barber will proudly announce a new chair from Kansas City— indicating the western push of industrial civilization). The proprietor has attempted to push his "barbershop" beyond the limits of the frontier, to comic effect. So it is entirely fitting that Wyatt's "quiet little shave" should be continually interrupted by a drunken Indian. Indian Joe's destructive actions demonstrate the corrupting forces of the frontier town on figures of the wilderness. Frontier towns in Ford films contain the explosive combination of the violently primitive and the righteously civilized. As a mediator Wyatt instinctively expects Tombstone to be more authentically civilized ("What kind of town is this, anyway?"). It is this incident that triggers the civilizing of Wyatt Earp. It's as though he must clean up the town to get a shave. Which is what makes his first step, the flushing out of Indian Joe with lather on his beard, so comical and so right.

The next step, after burying his youngest brother and accepting the job as town marshal, is to deal with that icon of the frontier town, the saloon. The narrative progression suggests that Wyatt will not get his "quiet little shave" until the saloon, and thus Doc Holliday (Victor Mature), have been domesticated. The culmination of this long process occurs when, with Doc's saloon singer girlfriend, Chihuahua's (Linda Darnell), life at stake, Doc attempts to return to his former civilized profession. Even the saloon's poker tables are transformed into an operating theater. Wyatt has been told that the Clantons control the cattle (the wilderness) and Doc runs the gambling (the frontier town). First Wyatt will have to drive the wilderness out of the frontier town, then he can confront the wilderness. Violence in the wilderness (his brother's death) and violence in the frontier town transform him from a wilderness/frontier town figure into the avatar of civilization. The first saloon scene is a brilliant example of Wyatt's civilizing powers: he tames the wild Chihuahua, intimidates the professional gambler, and wins Doc over without a gun. The frontier town may be civilized without a gun, but the wilderness won't. So Wyatt and his brothers will have to gun down the Clantons. Forceful persuasion is the mark of the Fordian mediating hero; violence is his last resort.

At the very moment Doc and Wyatt toast their uneasy alliance with champagne, a gesture of ironically civilized one-upmanship, the traveling tragedian, Granville Thorndyke (Alan Mowbray), appears with a flourish, announcing his performance of *Hamlet* at the theater. Doc says, wistfully, "Shakespeare in Tombstone. Been a long time since I've heard Shakespeare." Three civilizing factors have been involved in the saloon scene: the absence of a gun belt on Wyatt, the champagne, and Shakespeare. Only one of them, but the most important, was introduced by Wyatt. Civilization is inexorably on the march, and is beyond the control of any one person.

The central figure during this part of the film is Doc Holliday, a complexly drawn character who has escaped from Eastern civilization. Though he hates it, he is drawn back to it from time to time. Shakespeare's "To be or not to be" soliloquy returns him to his past and deeper self. But he will have to stumble upon it in a rough saloon, for the Clantons, those "tavern louts," have kidnapped the actor, thereby denying Tombstone Shakespeare's civilizing influence. Doc and Wyatt enter the saloon as the Clantons are forcing Thorndyke to recite "To be or not to be." Shakespeare's words take on a special meaning for Doc. Wyatt, who is suffering from no conscious identity crisis, watches as Doc takes over from the tragedian who can no longer endure the slings and arrows of tavern louts. The portion that Doc recites speaks volumes about Doc's tragedy and the West: "But that the dread of something after death, / The undiscover'd country from whose bourn / No traveller returns, puzzles the will / And makes us rather bear those ills we have / Than fly to others that we know not of? / Thus conscience does make cowards of us all." Doc is cut short by a consumptive coughing fit, foreshadowing his inevitable death in this undiscovered country.

Doc's life in the West has been a death wish. His East/West ambivalence shows in the civilized baggage he carries with him, the books, photographs, and diploma. He fails to save Chihuahua's life (a companion piece to Doc Boone's success in *Stagecoach*). She becomes the first of the wilderness figures to die. Doc regards his failure as the corruption of his civilized talents. He is the lost man of the West, doomed to die in the wilderness. His white handkerchief, a legacy of his civilized self, flutters over that Fordian boundary between wilderness and civilization, the wooden rail fence at the O. K. Corral.

Chihuahua and Doc die to make way for the rebirth of Wyatt and Clementine. Wyatt and Clementine are a mediating pair, like Dallas and Ringo in *Stagecoach* and Hallie and Ranse in *Liberty Valance*. Each has a partner who has moved toward the other from an opposite direction: Clementine, Dallas, and Ranse from civilization toward the wilderness; Wyatt, Ringo, and Hallie from the wilderness toward civilization. They all meet on the frontier.

Clementine's (Cathy Downs) introduction as the films' major civilizing factor has been carefully prepared. She enters after Wyatt's abortive shave, after the taming of the saloon, and after Shakespeare. Then, one clear morning as Wyatt relaxes in that feet-up way that signifies control, a stage arrives (the stagecoach is a major civilizing signifier in this film, though it is not in *Liberty Valance*). With quiet authority and physical grace Wyatt tells a gambler to be on the next stage out of town. But suddenly his sense of easy command comes unglued as this new civilizing force enters his sphere. He becomes a wilderness figure, all innocent, shy, and awkward. When Clementine steps off the stage, Ford introduces the "Clementine" theme, played, not as a Western tune as it had been in the credits, but as a piece of eighteenth-century chamber music in the same minuet style that opened the wedding scene in *Drums along the Mohawk*. This music effectively marks Clementine as an Eastern civilizing factor.

By the end of the film, however, both Wyatt's elegance and awkwardness are compressed into his shy kiss on Clementine's cheek and graceful ride into Monument Valley. Just as the saloon had symbolized the frontier town, and the barber pole the next level of civilization, Clementine's coming (another level) is symbolized by the emergence of saguaro cacti in Tombstone. Douglas Gomery in an extremely convincing close study of the film's mise-en-scène noticed that a saloon mysteriously disappeared, while just as mysteriously the cacti appeared where there had previously been none—precisely at the moment of civilizing transformations.[3] Rather than chalk this up to directorial sloppiness, Gomery views it as a brilliant example of Ford's creative manipulation of mise-en-scène. Gomery is right, of course, because the timing of the saloon's and barber pole's eclipse by the cacti is too carefully linked to Clementine's arrival.

My Darling Clementine has a civilizing centerpiece, the Sunday morning ritual (the equivalent of *Stagecoach's* childbirth event). From the haircut to the carving of the Sunday roast Wyatt (America) enters an era of mature community. This is the birth of a new civilization. As though to reinforce both its tragic and progressive implications this sequence is framed by instances of Doc's self-destructiveness. The gulf between Doc and Wyatt, frontier town and civilized community, has become unbridgeable. In the scene before the Sunday sequence Doc has told Clementine to go home: "This is no place for your kind of person." Then he goes up to his room, and, in another of Ford's privileged moments of pastness, sees himself reflected in his diploma. In a rage he shatters the glass, as if to destroy both his past and his present. Ford gives us visual confirmation of what Doc had earlier told Clementine against the darkening light of the wilderness: "The man you once knew is no more. There's not a vestige of him left. Nothing."

After the Sunday community ritual, at which Doc's absence is so conspicuous, Doc storms down the hotel stairs disrupting Wyatt's paterfamilias meat carving. Doc demands to know why Clementine has not left town. For the first time Wyatt displays the touch of holier-than-thou moral righteousness that is so endemic to civilized societies: "Miss Carter or any other decent citizen can stay here just as long as they want to." Is this smugness the price that must be paid for civilization? Does civilization inevitably lead to the "foul disease called social prejudice" that Boone spoke of in *Stagecoach*? Ford seems ambivalent about it all.

The Sunday morning sequence is one of film history's great tours de force. It is so right, rich, and real that one almost smells and feels the clean, fresh desert air. It is one of those rare experiences in art when one's entire being is so transported into the imaginative sphere that it becomes real. The day begins with a slow procession of wagons into town and a huge saguaro cactus prominently displayed in the foreground. The scene immediately shifts to the barber proudly revealing to Wyatt his slicked-down handiwork. The farmers and settlers continue to pour into Tombstone past the open door of the barbershop. All the signifiers of a domesticated West are on display: the barber in his starched white coat, the new barber chair, the mirror, the fancy lettering for the fancy Bon Ton Tonsorial Parlor, Wyatt's dark dress suit and new hat, his missing gunbelt, and the families in buckboards and wagons. Wyatt is enclosed within a puzzling and disorienting interior space. When he looks in the mirror at the Tonsorial Parlor, he is not sure what he sees. Just moments earlier Doc also was not sure what he saw in the reflected glass of his diploma. Their identities are changing and crossing. Doc slides toward primitive self-destruction, while Wyatt strides toward becoming a "decent citizen." Wyatt's quizzical expression suggests that he barely recognizes this new self.

In a brilliantly conceived shot the barber holds the mirror up for both the audience and Wyatt to see. What is outside the frame of the mirror is the disoriented real world with its inside-out lettering of the Tonsorial Parlor and disembodied figure of the barber holding the mirror. The mirror, ironically enough, reveals the civilized world as coherent with readable lettering and spatial context. As Wyatt walks out of the Tonsorial Parlor, all coiffed and reeking of "that sweet smelling stuff," he takes one last look at himself in the reflection of a store window. His unreflected self is framed against the mercantile world of civilization, while his reflected self, featureless in silhouette, stands against the wilderness. The wilderness is now behind Wyatt.

A moment later he is performing his famous tilting-chair, right-foot-left-foot-against-the-post balancing act. This is the performance of an integrated personality. Chihuahua recedes into the background in this

Wyatt Earp (Henry Fonda) becoming civilized: the new image of his coiffeured self reflects the righted world, while his old world is backwards (top); the windows of civilization reflect the wilderness, now in back of Wyatt (bottom).

scene. When Wyatt walks into the hotel lobby softly whistling "My Darling Clementine," Clementine Carter, that civilizing factor of the future, is sitting in the foreground waiting for the stage to take her back East. Doc has renounced her and she has given up her goal of returning him to Eastern civilization. But the bell of the skeletal church begins to chime. Clementine echoes Doc's "Shakespeare in Tombstone" line when she says, "I believe that's the first church bell I've heard in months." Shakespeare caught up with Doc; now church bells have penetrated the West. As Clementine stands on the porch taking in what she thinks is the rich scent of the desert flower, Wyatt sheepishly admits, "That's me—barber." This is the perfect fusion of wilderness and civilization, for even this artificially civilized scent seems to blend in with the desert.

The voices of the community sing, "Shall We Gather at the River," and Clementine indicates that she would like to attend church with Wyatt. Taken aback, he blurts out in his most courtly manner, "Yes, ma'm. I'd admire to take you." Wyatt has become ensnared in unnatural, civilized language. This kind of comic moment filled with meaning has always been one of Ford's strengths. As Clementine and Wyatt walk arm in arm down the wooden sidewalk past the barbershop, the barber pole, remarkably enough, is missing (it has not been removed from its location; instead, the camera angles have carefully shaven it out of the frame). The barber and his pole have been left behind, a poignant vestige of frontier town upward mobility. Wyatt and Clementine walk, almost with destiny in their eyes and gait, toward the new civilization of bells, singing, American flags, church, and dance.

As they continue toward the sound of the singing, the camera, which had been tracking in front of them, watching the town recede into the distance, suddenly switches to a reverse angle, revealing the skeletal church rising from the desert, as if some sacred fount had been reborn in the wilderness. Two American flags flutter in the cool spring breeze, one waiting to be changed to a state flag—a process that will have to wait until *Liberty Valance*. After a few perspectives on this structure and gathering, Ford holds the shot that crystallizes the entire film's vision of civilization. In a long, slightly high-angle shot from foreground to background stand the ingredients of the long march of civilization: the people, the flag, the church, the frontier town, and a mesa of the wilderness. People, the essence of any civilization, are in the foreground. Slender but towering stand the incipient structures of the new civilization. In the distance the frontier town looks forgotten, but through the haze of the far distance a solid, powerful, unchanging mesa refuses to disappear. This composition, perhaps the most brilliant of Ford's career, gives visual majesty and coherence to his myth of American civilization.

Three levels of American civilization in one shot: the wilderness, the frontier town, and civilization.

Ford's ultimate expression of community cohesion, a dance, begins on the floor of the unfinished church, thus sealing civilization's compact. Wyatt, still the outsider, looks uncomfortable. Finally, he tosses his hat away (in a gesture of sexual release that John Wayne will repeat six years later in *The Quiet Man*) and asks Clementine to dance. He takes her wrap and bows in an awkward but courtly manner. Two saguaro cacti stand between them in the distance at this moment; presumably the second is emblematic of the newly civilized Wyatt. Fonda's famous dance style (introduced in *Young Mr. Lincoln*) expresses both his awkward civilized self and his untutored natural self. A short time later Wyatt is presiding over the ritual Sunday dinner with the same authority as Mr. Morgan had in *How Green Was My Valley*. Wyatt's family is becoming the church-going community of Tombstone.

But Doc interrupts the consummation of this ritual, forcing Wyatt back into the wilderness to complete his unfinished family business. The Clantons have been virtually forgotten in Wyatt's love affair with civilization. The corrupt forces of the wilderness have not been disposed of; Wyatt has not been fully tested; and the vengeance cycle has not yet run its course. Wyatt learns that Doc gave Chihuahua the medallion that was stolen from Wyatt's murdered brother. Believing Doc to be the killer, Wyatt rides after him in one of cinema's great crosscut chase scenes. Wyatt and Doc finally meet in the same frame, with the promise of a classical shoot-out (in his sound pictures Ford never produced a clichéd shoot-out). Wyatt, with enough of the wilderness left in him (*he* rides the horse, while Doc rides the stage), is able to outshoot Doc, yet civilized enough not to kill him. Doc is not James Earp's killer, of course. Billy Clanton had given James's medallion to Chihuahua. She and Doc, the two transitional figures of the wilderness and frontier town, are gunned down by the most primitive forces of the wilderness, the Clantons.

Doc is found to be expendable in the final wilderness-civilization confrontation. The famous gunfight at O. K. Corral occurs on the edge of the newly civilized Tombstone. Aided by a passing stagecoach (civilization), the last vestiges of the wilderness are destroyed. But Wyatt, so civilized he is willing to let old man Clanton live and wander[11] for a hundred years, becomes a vulnerable target for this last old warrior of the wilderness. Wyatt's brother kills Clanton just in time. Finally, both clean-shaven and wearing his old wilderness coat, Wyatt leaves for California, promising Clementine he will return. Wyatt and the West are not so completely tamed that they are ready, just yet, to settle down. This time he and his one remaining brother, Morgan (Ward Bond), take a buckboard with them. The buckboard, the shave, the fence, and the kiss on the cheek of the new schoolmarm all indicate the civilizing of the wilderness. Still, Wyatt rides off into the land of prehistoric mesas, unable to completely slough off the remains of the wilderness that gave him the power to become a frontier hero in the first place. Perhaps he returns to the wilderness to rejuvenate his spirit, to keep in touch with the source of his strength, to drink at the fount of America's secret heart.

The Man Who Shot Liberty Valance (1962)

Some years later in John Ford's mythic American civilization, Tombstone has become Shinbone, the last frontier town. Ford was fifty-one years old when he made *Clementine* and sixty-seven when he made *The Man Who Shot Liberty Valance*. In *Liberty Valance* Ford's difference in age shows. In his mythic chronology Wyatt Earp in the prime of his life stood between the eternal hero of the Old West, Tom Doniphon (John Wayne), and the aging progenitor of the new West, Ransom Stoddard (James Stewart), embodying the positive qualities of both eras. He was the flexible mediator of the frontier's zenith. In *The Man Who Shot Liberty Valance* Ford cast a more jaundiced eye on the frontier progression that had once looked so promising in *Clementine*.

Liberty Valance's flashback structure allowed Ford to place the West's past and modern present (its future, metaphorically) in perspective. Ford's decision to shoot the film in black and white in 1962 produced a dark, anachronistic look, while the blatant soundstage effects of the film's opening scene, the stagecoach holdup, reinforced Ford's vision of a wildernessless, interiorized West. Doniphon and Liberty Valance (Lee Marvin) stand as the benevolent and malevolent surrogates of the vanished landscape. Liberty lives "where I hang my hat" and Tom lives "out Desert Way." Liberty, as his name indicates, tries to hang on to the freedom of the wilderness, while Tom tries to make the transition to civilization. Both efforts are doomed. Liberty is shot down in the town he wanted to liberate; Tom, having killed the symbol of the wilderness, burns down the house that symbolized his frontier domestication. He even releases the horses from the corral. This dialectical structure highlights Ford's ambivalence about civilization's "progress."

The world of the frame tale, the modern, turn-of-the-century Shinbone, seems lonely and mercenary without the guiding principles and emotions that Hallie (Vera Miles) and Ranse could bring to it. By the end of the film (also in the frame tale) they have decided to return to Shinbone, whether to save it or themselves we are not sure. Hallie and Ranse return to the modern Shinbone neither on horseback nor by stagecoach, but in a train that billows black smoke out over the tamed, verdant landscape. The frontier (if it is still that) has been pushed beyond the reach of the primordial Monument Valley.

Civilized Shinbone is introduced through a low-angle shot that frames the aged, forlorn, and isolated Link Appleyard (Andy Devine) against a tall, modern building. His expression as he waits for Hallie and Ranse suggests that he expects two saviors who will deliver him from the pain of this mercenary civilization. For instance, when a young reporter calls his editor upon learning that Ranse is an important politician, the stationmaster impersonally yells, "Hey, bub, that's a nickel." And Clute, the undertaker, has already stripped Tom's corpse of his gun belt and boots.

Loneliness dominates the darkened back room in which Tom's coffin rests. Pompey (Woody Strode), Tom's black hired hand, sits broken and humbled. But loneliest of all is the plain pine box holding the forgotten hero of the Old West. Gone is the crowded kitchen and teeming dining room of Pete's Place, the colorful drunkenness of Dutton Peabody (Edmond O'Brien), the editor of the *Shinbone Star*, and the marvelously chaotic election held in the saloon. People, all kinds of people, were the essence of the frontier Shinbone. They got in each other's way, fought, argued, and teased, but always showed tolerance toward each other. The new Shinbone cries out for people. Where have they gone? The town is empty of people. Civilization usually has been characterized as too crowded, but Ford turned that convention around by depicting modern society as literally depersonalized. Why, then, do Hallie and Ranse want to return? Because "my roots are here," says Hallie. Because Shinbone is less civilized than their present abode, Washington, D.C. And, perhaps, because Hallie and Ranse could help restore some of Shinbone's frontier qualities.

The romance in Ford's soul may have longed for the good old days, but by turning Liberty Valance and his henchmen into evil sociopaths, Ford made nostalgia difficult to swallow whole. How could one rationalize the violence of that era? The dialectic of the film is, therefore, not the wonderful past opposed to the awful present, but the violent past juxtaposed against the tepid present, the peopled past against the empty present, the anarchistic past against the democratic present. Both the past and the present have positive and negative qualities.

This relationship is clearly shown by the two scenes on either side of the flashback: the first occurs in the office of the modern *Shinbone Star* where Ranse is telling the story of Shinbone's old days; the second shows the beginning of the tale with Valance's stagecoach robbery and Ranse's ignoble entry into Shinbone. In the first instance, Ranse finds himself in conflict with the modern editor of the *Shinbone Star*. The editor demands that Ranse reveal why he returned to Shinbone. Ranse is being bullied by a principle he believes in, the public's right to knowledge concerning the actions of public personalities. The conflict between public rights and invasion of privacy, so crucial to Ford's late films, surfaces in its most extreme form here. It is Hallie who first recognizes the worth of this right; she gives her approval and Ranse relents.

Ranse's tale is triggered by a dusty, old stagecoach, the one that brought Ranse out West. And, metaphorically speaking, this is the same stage that delivered Clementine in *My Darling Clementine* to Tombstone and transported that odd band of travelers from Tonto to Lordsburg in *Stagecoach*. In Ford's mythic world the horse is the symbol of the wilderness, the covered wagon stands for the new frontier, the stage for the frontier town, the buckboard for family civilization, and the train for urban civilization. Ranse removes a layer of dust both from the stage and the past, and begins the tale of the man who shot Liberty Valance. Ranse walks out of the frame, leaving only the stage. Then, through the shortest of dissolves, the stagecoach, is transported into a dangerous, dark, wilderness landscape. But his landscape is a studio soundstage. So when Valance tells the stagecoach driver to "stand and deliver," the tinny, artificial sound has the effect of a bad dream. It is Ranse's dream of the past.

Valance only wants to rob the stage. Instead, he finds himself maniacally tearing up law books and beating Ranse senseless because

Ranse represents Valance's greatest fear, civilization. Valance must trample on all of Ranse's Eastern baggage: chivalry, books, and law. It is Valance's anti-Gutenbergian rages that motivate, at the deepest psychological level, Ranse's decision to tell his story to the editor. Print is the vehicle for education; law is the enemy of anarchy; and chivalry is the behavioral code of civilization. Ranse embodies all three.

The dream of civilization envisions a progression from violence to peace, but in Ford's frontier mythos progress also means the inclusion of increasingly malevolent wilderness figures: for instance, the Clantons in *Clementine*, the Cleggs in *Wagon Master*, and Liberty Valance all display sociopathic tendencies, whereas the Indians in many Westerns and the Plummers in *Stagecoach* are viewed essentially as combatants. This vision of frontiers beset by wilderness sociopaths conforms to the gangster and detective genres' proposition that cities have become the modern frontiers, the urban "jungles." Dark though *Liberty Valance* may be, it does not approach the hellish, nightmare world of urban *noir* films. Ford never really confronted the end of the cycle. He could not and did not indulge in dead-end despair.

Liberty Valance has a complex light-dark structure. Many of the flashback scenes are shrouded in darkness, whereas the frame tale is bathed in light. This belies the "good old days" approach so often read into this film. As in *noir* films, darkness both arouses and cloaks violence: Valance steps out of the darkness to hold up the stage; Peabody lights the lantern revealing Valance ready to destroy his printing presses; Tom shoots Valance from the dark alley. Modern Shinbone, however, is all sunlight, save for that back room where Tom's coffin lies. This room becomes the link between the flashback and the frame tale. Darkness signifies the death of the frontier and the memory of that vibrant era. The darkness is ambivalent. In *My Darling Clementine* Wyatt changed from man of the wilderness to frontier town marshal, to civilized member of society (though not fully achieved). Wyatt was the holistic hero of the sun-drenched West. Ford stretched Wyatt's mediating capabilities as far as he could. The mythic world of *Clementine* is unified by the continuity of its middle position. *Liberty Valance* depicts greater extremes. It is a divided frontier where the wilderness and civilization cannot be contained in one man. This lack of unity, produces the tragic tone of *Liberty Valance*, just as it did in *Fort Apache*.

This division in *Liberty Valance* also produces a more complex structure of human relationships with respect to conflict, mediation, and fusion. This structure exists on three levels: the physical (as characters are positioned within the mise-en-scène), the psychological, and the mythical. For instance, Tom and Ranse often physically confront each other, with either no one else in the frame or no one positioned between them. These confrontations tend to revolve around their psychological struggle for Hallie's love. And at the same time these confrontations represent conflicting stages in the myth of American civilization: Tom is the wilderness frontiersman, while Ranse is the civilized frontiersman; Tom is the cowboy-small rancher and Ranse is the educated professional; Tom can no longer change with the times, while Ranse represents the beginning of new changes; Tom remains associated with the pastness of the wilderness, while Ranse represents the future of civilization; Tom is a confronter and Ranse is a mediator. These structural configurations also apply to the other two dominant characters, Hallie and Liberty Valance. Valance is a confronter, like Tom, but he is more completely associated with the wilderness. He has not made the change Tom did to associate himself with the frontier, small ranching. His fight is with Ranse, who represents everything that will destroy his world. Hallie, along with Ranse, is characterized as a mediator. As a woman in an American civilization film, she is a civilizing factor, just as Clementine Carter had been in *My Darling Clementine*. In the beginning of the tale it is made quite clear that Hallie is Tom's girl—at this point he represents Shinbone's most civilized hero. But when Ranse arrives, Tom understands what neither Hallie nor Ranse do, that a struggle has begun for the leap to a new, more civilized stage of frontier culture. And Hallie is the prize, since she as a woman represents the frontier's eternal civilizing factor. It is significant, then, that on both a psychological and a mythical level Hallie cannot fully commit herself to Ranse until he has stood up to Liberty Valance. He must prove himself to be the frontier hero of the next stage of American civilization.

The ironies that are built into the question of who shot Liberty Valance reverberate throughout the film on many levels. The legend, that Ranse shot Liberty, determined that Hallie would marry Ranse, that Ranse would lead the frontier toward a new level of civilization, and that he would become a figure of national and international importance. Meanwhile Tom would lose Hallie and become the forgotten man of the frontier's wilderness stage. This legend also meant that Hallie would learn to read and write and see "real" roses. All this was made possible because it was actually Tom who killed Liberty in, as Tom himself admits, "cold-blooded murder." Without this admission Ranse would have returned to the East during the territorial convention believing that he could not be civilization's leader since he would have had "blood on his hands." The legend makes Ranse's heroic position in society possible, while the fact releases him from debilitating guilt. At the same time the legend consigns Tom to oblivion, while the fact burdens him with the guilt; "but I can live with it," he says. Tom knowingly sacrifices himself for the future and the march of civilization. He is the tragic wilderness hero of *The Man Who Shot Liberty Valance*, while Ranse is its humane civilization hero. Violence, both in legend and in fact, has determined their destinies.

The structural basis on which this film is grounded—conflict, mediation, and fusion—is most graphically represented by the carefully choreographed positionings and movements of the four central characters within the close quarters of this diminished frontier. There are three basic conflicts: 1) Tom versus Ranse; 2) Tom versus Valance; 3) Valance versus Ranse. In each case there is a provocateur, the one who is spoiling for a fight. In the first two conflicts it is Tom, and in the third it is Valance. The message that becomes apparent through a structural analysis of the conflicts is that the provocateurs cannot become mediators. Neither Tom nor Valance is ever placed in mediating positions, that is, found holding the center of a three-person configuration within the same frame. Their usual approach is to burst into a two-person relationship, friendly or antagonistic, and attempt to thrust themselves into the middle of it—as though hoping to establish themselves as mediators. But they always fail, because one of the original two always disappears from the frame, leaving the intruding antagonist in a conflicting rather than a mediating position.

Then there are the mediating configurations. Again, there are three of them, with the mediator in the middle position: 1) Tom-Hallie-Ranse; 2) Valance-Ranse-Tom; 3) Hallie-Ranse-Tom. The two mediators are Hallie and Ranse, and it is these two who provide finally the fusion. They are continually shown in nonconflicting two-shots throughout the film, most notably at the end of the film when both Valance and Tom are dead and buried. It is important to remember that in each physical configuration of conflict, mediation, and fusion there is a simultaneous psychological and mythical reading of that configuration.

In the beginning of the film, both in the frame tale and in Ranse's tale, the first mediating triangle, the Tom-Hallie-Ranse one, is dominant. For instance, the film's first three-shot of them is as Hallie and Ranse enter the room where Tom's coffin rests. Hallie is in the central mediating position. At the end of the film when they leave the room, by contrast, Ranse will be in the center of this configuration. The thrust of the film is progressively to make Ranse the more dominant mediator. Hallie can mediate the conflicts between Tom and Ranse, both the psychological (two men vying for the same woman) and the mythical (benevolent wilderness frontiersman versus benevolent civilization frontiersman). But she is not cast in the role of civilization's leader. She is its facilitator and then Ranse's partner. She is the transitional figure, the bridge between the world of Tom and the world of Ranse.

Hallie's space is the kitchen of the restaurant. It is here that she tends Ranse when he is brought into town, though Tom quickly takes over, thrusting Hallie out of the frame. It is in this kitchen that all of Hallie's mediating is done and where a basic pattern of fusion, mediation, and conflict occurs. Ranse and Hallie are usually framed together (Ranse works as a dishwasher and sleeps on a cot in the kitchen); Tom enters and attempts to push himself between Hallie and Ranse, and into a conflict with Ranse. For a moment the three of them are framed together with Hallie in the middle, then Hallie is removed from the frame, leaving Tom and Ranse in conflict. When Hallie reenters the frame she is in a mediating position. She and Tom then are framed together until, and almost invariably, Tom leaves. Each time he departs it represents a more definitive breach in their relationship. Hallie is usually framed alone at the end of these scenes. This pattern seems to indicate that Hallie's position as a mediator isolates her more than Ranse's does.

Ranse's first moment of mediation occurs during the steak-picking-up scene, which should be considered the film's pivotal point. If Tom and Ranse are in conflict, Valance and Ranse are at war. There can be no reconciliation. So when Valance has a chance to further humiliate "the new waitress," he trips Ranse, and Tom's steak falls to the floor. Tom uses the pretext that it was his steak to confront Valance. These two are natural antagonists, as well. For though they are both wilderness figures (which is why Valance does not wish to fight Tom), Tom sees in Valance the malevolence of an unchanging wilderness sociopath who should be destroyed so the frontier can survive unmolested. So Tom and Valance fill the frames for a moment, while Ranse is on the floor. Death seems to be a certainty in this confrontation. But Ranse, rejecting violence as the only solution, rises from the floor between Valance and Tom and throws the steak on the plate, saying, "What's the matter? Is everybody in this country kill-crazy? There! There! Now— it's picked up!" Ranse demonstrates that he is civilization's mediator by stopping the violence. But the "one measly steak" is not the issue, and Ranse does not yet understand this. Finally he will have to resort to violence, to "the gun," because on the frontier such a clash between the wilderness and civilization can be settled in no other way—the wilderness representatives will see to that. Because he both rejects violence and is willing to confront it and because, as he says after the steak incident, "Nobody fights my battles," he is capable of being the frontier mediator. This incident shows that Ranse is capable of mediation, and the triangular configuration reinforces this view, whereas the mise-en-scène does not support Tom's view of himself as

Tom Doniphon (John Wayne) forces himself into the mediating position between Hallie (Vera Miles) and Ranse (James Stewart) early in Liberty Valance *(top); Ranse is in a mediating position, off-screen, between Valance (Lee Marvin), who threatens him, and Doniphon (bottom).*

mediating between Valance and Ranse. Tom's actions are those of a confronter.

The same is true of Liberty Valance. During Shinbone's election for representatives to the territorial convention, Valance actually attempts to have himself elected. But he is defeated both by parliamentary procedure and democratic vote. Valance has been done in by civilization's procedures, and he knows who to blame. As he comes at Ranse, Tom again tries to shift the fight to himself. This time Valance will have none of it: "You stay out of this, Doniphon. He's been hiding behind your gun long enough." Suddenly, what for a moment had been a triad with Valance in the middle shifts to a subjective camera shot. Valance is standing next to Tom pointing offscreen toward Ranse/the camera and saying, "You be there [on the street tonight, alone], and don't make us come get ya." Valance has forced the confrontation, but by keeping Ranse in a subjective offscreen position, he also maintains the integrity of Ranse's mediating role. It is important to note that all the encounters Ranse has with Valance are shot from a strong subjective point of view. It is as though Ford believed that since this is Ranse's tale, his most vulnerable moments should take on a more personal tone. These would be the times Ranse would be unable to maintain his pose as omniscient storyteller: on the ground during the holdup; entering the dining room with an apron on; being warned during the election; and the moment before Valance is about to shoot him.

The two shoot-out scenes are the most telling with respect to Ford's manipulation of mise-en-scène for the purposes of establishing Ranse as a mediator and not an antagonist. In the first version of the inevitable shoot-out (where Ranse appears to shoot Liberty) our perspective is limited by Ranse's limited perspective. The force of the event is so strong that we accept Ranse's version that has him finally, positioned, in a confrontational role. Perhaps there was the nagging question, where is Tom? Perspective and desire overwhelm mythical logic (perhaps even physical and psychological logic, as well. Can we really believe that the wounded Ranse could have shot Valance with his left hand, and with his "popgun"?). The mythical logic of this film demands that Ranse maintain his position as civilization's mediator—so Ranse's version of the shoot-out fails: first, because he is not physically in his appointed middle position and, second because as civilization's representative he cannot kill a man.

Tom's version, therefore, restores Ranse on both counts. This second version shows us the scene from Tom's point of view, but with him visible to the audience. The camera angle has Tom on the left in the foreground with Ranse in the middle and Valance on the right in the background. Now we can see Ranse's and Tom's guns fire simultaneously. Ranse has not shot Liberty Valance. Everything in this film favors Ranse; he is allowed to have his cake and eat it, too. Why?

Because mythical logic has tapped him to lead civilization out of the wilderness, just as it has decreed that Tom Doniphon will become expendable.

One final mediating configuration is due Ranse. Tom has made it possible for Ranse to lead the frontier into the era of railroads and cities, to create a history. "Hallie's your girl, now," says Tom after his version of the shoot-out. "You taught her how to read and write. Now give her something to read and write about." Ranse returns to accept the nomination, and the rest is, shall we say, history. Tom, however, has the doors of history shut behind him as he disappears into obscurity. So, in the frame tale Ranse has come west to pay a final, private tribute to a forgotten man. With prodding he reveals the role Tom played, in an effort to restore him to the pages of history. But the modern newspaper editor, who we could argue knows nothing of the West, crumples up the history he has just recorded and throws it into the fire, reconsigning Tom Doniphon to oblivion. Turning to Ranse, he says, "This is the West, sir. When the legend becomes fact, print the legend." John Ford, the romancer, has printed both the fact and the legend, the real and the marvelous.

A train whistle blows, breaking the trance of the past and signalling the end of Ranse's and Hallie's stay in Shinbone. Ranse returns to the back room where Tom's corpse has been lying throughout this tale with his true wilderness frontier compatriots, Pompey, Link, and Hallie. As Ranse and Hallie leave, they are framed in the doorway with Tom's coffin. Now we see the final mediating configuration: deep in the background stands Hallie; Ranse is in the doorway at middle ground; and Tom's coffin rests in the foreground. This is a new and more difficult relationship for Ranse to mediate, the love that Hallie and Tom had for each other. For the last time the door is shut on Tom. He is now alone with Hallie's gesture of love, and the frontier's—the cactus rose. The camera moves in slightly, giving emphasis to this sacred object which is now bathed in an almost metaphysical stream of sunlight. The "Ann Rutledge theme" plays softly over this moment, not the expected theme that had been associated with Tom, the theme that had been played dirgelike when Hallie and Ranse first saw the coffin.

The musical themes reinforce both the conflicts and the fusion inherent in this film. Ford's reuse of the "Ann Rutledge theme" from *Young Mr. Lincoln* has been much commented upon. But David Coursen's analysis is especially astute: "The music is invariably linked to an ideal, promised or remembered . . . thus, in the past the music registers a hope for the future, and in the present regret at the loss of the past."[4] This observation, though, is in relation to audience reaction and makes no distinction between the film's three musical themes. The "Ann Rutledge theme" is lyrical and primarily associated with Hallie.

Ranse in the final mediating position as civilization's hero, between Tom in the coffin and Hallie in the background.

It becomes the film's "civilization theme." The more strident Western-like theme which is played during the credits and seems to be the film's signature music is actually associated with Tom and becomes the "wilderness theme." And thirdly, there is the Mexican-style music which, based on its location and recurrence in earlier Ford civilization films, can be identified as "frontier town music." This music is not as melodically thematic and not as evocatively important, but it does stand as a musical signature for that stage of American civilization that is both wild and peopled. It is the music of the saloon world.

The "wilderness theme" opens and closes the film. During the credits it is insistent, whereas its final appearance, after both the "Ann Rutledge theme" (which I will henceforth refer to as the "civilization theme") and "The End," is more mellow and lyrical—as though having been fused to the inherently more lyrical "civilization theme." Through the telling of this tale in which Tom Doniphon is remembered as the sacrificial hero and facilitator of civilization and through the fusion of the legend with the fact, these two musical themes have come as close as possible to being one.

This is not the case during the film, however. David Coursen is right that the "Ann Rutledge/civilization theme" looks both toward the past and the future. And it is this that helps explain why Ford returned to *Young Mr. Lincoln* for this musical signature. It was Ann who motivated Lincoln to become civilization's leader, propelling him into the future, and when he was on his way there his memories of Ann were always indicated by the playing of that theme. Much the same effect is created by this musical theme in *Liberty Valance*. This "civilization theme" occurs seven times during the film with Hallie as the one constant. Three of those instances are in the present tense of the frame tale. Two of these, one at the beginning and one at the end, are associated with the cactus rose that Hallie gathers at Tom's burned-out ranch to place on Tom's plain pine coffin. And the third occurs at the end of the film right after the train conductor has just told Ranse that "nothing's too good for the man who shot Liberty Valance." Since we now know who did shoot Liberty Valance, the irony of that statement sends the audience's and Ranse's thoughts back into the past. Hallie, who has been preoccupied for some time, is presumably already lost in the past (whether she knows who shot Liberty Valance is unknown, thereby providing a complex of subtle tensions at this moment: Does Hallie know that Ranse is not the heroic destroyer of Valance? Does she not know? Would it make a difference to her if she did know?, etc.). Therefore, each of the three frame tale instances of the "civilization theme" evokes associations with Tom and the past. Still, there is one missing ingredient—the fact that the cactus rose and the killing of Valance are civilizing factors. So, in the frame tale this musical theme evokes both a pastness and a futureness, just as it did in *Young Mr. Lincoln*.

During the tale itself, the four remaining instances of this theme are closely associated with civilizing factors: the first occurs when Hallie tells Ranse she would like to learn to read; the second happens when Hallie is looking at the cactus rose Tom has just given her, but Ranse asks her if she has ever seen a real rose; the third instance is in the classroom after Tom has left, throwing doubt on the future of schooling in Shinbone so long as Valance is alive; and the fourth fully weds Hallie to Ranse because it emerges after Ranse has "shot" Liberty Valance and is being tended to by Hallie. Though Ranse was always present during these musical moments, the focus during the first three was on other civilizing factors (a rose or learning), but in the fourth instance Ranse alone embodies the civilizing factor. And it is at this moment that their mutual sexual attraction, which had been either repressed or suppressed by them throughout the tale, emerges. This musical theme has progressively indicated Hallie's movement away from Tom and the wilderness and toward Ranse and civilization. And this last scene physically, psychologically, and mythically unifies Hallie and

Ranse as civilization's twin representatives and mediators.

A moment later Tom enters, finding Hallie and Ranse in each other's arms, and at that instant the "civilization theme" changes to the "wilderness theme," played slowly and forcefully. This is the fourth of its six playings. Except for its first appearance, during the credits, all are closely associated with Tom. And with that exception, all are played at a certain slow, melancholy pace, belying the promised rousing Western action of its first playing during the credits. There it seemed to indicate it would be the film's theme song. But with its first appearance in the film proper, as Hallie and Ranse first set eyes on Tom's coffin in the frame tale, the theme is played as a dirge. In each of the three subsequent playings of this theme in Ranse's tale it is associated in an ever-increasing way with Tom's loss of Hallie: when Hallie calls Tom to teach Ranse to shoot; when Tom walks in on Hallie and Ranse after the first version of the shoot-out; and finally during Tom's telling of his version of the shoot-out.

This last instance is the most devastating, for now Tom is a broken man, unshaven and disheveled, who has lost his girl and his prominent position in the fast-changing society. He has insured his demise by shooting Valance. So the "wilderness theme" is a theme of loss and death, and as such it points in a direction that is for the most part opposed to the "civilization theme." Where they converge is in the final episode of the frame tale. Here both musical themes return us to the past and mourn its passing.

The music, then, helps to reinforce the film's (and Ford's) deep-seated ambiguity toward the loss of the wilderness and the march of civilization: before the frontier has been civilized (in Ranse's tale) there are positive responses toward civilization and the civilizing factors, but after the frontier has been civilized (in the frame tale) there are negative responses toward what civilization has wrought, and a yearning for the wilderness frontier of the past. By developing a narrative with a double perspective the creators of this film were able to address a fundamental human response, a simultaneous hope for the future and nostalgia for the past. It is also important to remember that at the end of the film Hallie and Ranse decide to return to this overcivilized Shinbone; for, having lived in the even more civilized East, they are still able to see Shinbone as a *frontier*. A frontier is always defined by one's point of view. *The Man Who Shot Liberty Valance* is a modernist film that acknowledges that relativism; whereas *My Darling Clementine* is a film of mythical utopianism that depicts the perfect, eternal frontier.

At the end of *Liberty Valance*, after Hallie and Ranse have decided to return to Shinbone, Hallie looks out of the train window and says, "Look at it—it was once a wilderness; now it's a garden. Aren't you

proud?" Ranse doesn't answer, knowing that he must share that pride
with the Tom Doniphons of the wilderness frontier, those forgotten
heroes who made the garden possible. It was the fusion of the wilderness and civilization as well as the conflict that created that garden.
This garden is simply a more civilized stage of the frontier—both for
better and for worse.

6

Narrative Structure: *Stagecoach* and *The Searchers*

FORD'S FILMS SET acknowledged standards for classical Hollywood narrative technique. Good narratives are far more complex than mere plot structures. *How* a story is told holds the key to its narrative success. Ford was actively interested in the crafting of his film's narratives. Many of his films were based on successful stories, plays, and novels. So the essential narrative foundations, though literary, were sound. Ford and his screenwriters always took liberties with the original's structure. The narrative structures of Ford's films are so similar and so consciously crafted that one must conclude that they are an intrinsic part of his style. Since narrative critical theory has firmly established that narrative techniques lie at the center of the creative consciousness, I believe it is important to show graphically, as well as expositorially, the narrative methods of two representative Ford films.[1]

I have chosen two films rather than one so as to counter the possibility that one film might prove to be an exception. My main criterion was to select representative films from Ford's pre– and post–World War II periods in order to give a more systematic expression to the critical controversy over his postwar changes. I have settled on two Westerns, *Stagecoach* and *The Searchers*, because each is an embodiment of the two periods critics are arguing about and because, finally, it is the Western that is most closely identified with Ford's towering reputation and where he seemed most free to express himself. I want to make it clear, however, that the conclusions I reach concerning Ford's Western narrative structures could as easily be reached about his non-Westerns.

The method for this chapter is a blending of both the graphic and the expository. Tables 1 and 2 will show the narrative structure of each film, followed by the conclusions that can be drawn from such a comparison. This process will be repeated in the side-by-side comparison of the films' narrative aspects in table 3. I have chosen sequences to be the basic structural unit of the tables. I reluctantly rejected various syntagmatic units used in various semiotic studies as too technical and

The mythical hero as outsider: John Wayne against Monument Valley in The Searchers.

cumbersome for this work. And the unit of scene is impractical because there are too many short scenes to be discussed adequately in one chapter. The structural clarity of these films would be lost in the minutiae of scene-by-scene analyses. Finally, after close study of the two films I am convinced that Ford and his screenwriters consciously used sequence as their basic structural unit for conveying each narrative's content.

Since rhythm is so crucial to narrative structure, I have attempted to demonstrate diachronically (across time) how Ford controlled each film's rhythm. The most obvious element is the running time of each sequence in relation to those preceding and subsequent to it. I have tried to represent graphically this aspect by spacing each sequence so as to approximate its running time. Another element of rhythm is editing. I have counted the number of shots within each sequence and divided that figure by the number of seconds. The result is an average per-second shot length for each sequence. The tempo and thematic coding of a film's music further contribute to its rhythm. Synchronically (vertical analysis during a given sequence), action and setting support the rhythms of a film's deeper structures, such as function and mythic discourse. For instance, the action of each sequence is clearly defined by the way it sustains the essential patterns of journey and quest tales. Action and setting combine to produce the essential signifiers of the mise-en-scène, while function joins with action and setting to generate the narrative's story and theme. Each sequence's action, setting, and function combine with the rhythmic forces that diachronically drive a film from one sequence to another and synchronically engender the deepest structure, which in Ford's case I have identified as mythic discourse. By noting the relationships between the vertical, synchronic elements (action, setting, function, etc.) and the patterns they form on the horizontal, diachronic level we can draw conclusions about the formal unity of these films from Ford's two major periods.

Tables 1 and 2 demonstrate that there were a number of structural principles that remained unchanged from 1939 to 1956: symmetry, overtures and codas, fulcrum midpoints, and alternating rhythms. Ford's and his screenwriters' use of symmetry never wavered. The practice of it went beyond mere beginnings and endings. It extended into the deepest recesses of the whole narrative. The climaxes (defined here as the penultimate sequences) and codas (the final sequences) are not mere repetitions of the overtures (the first sequence). In both films the actions of the overtures and the codas take place on the frontier. The frontier is both dichotomized (through setting) and unified (through action). At the same time, the narrative direction of both films demands that the codas reverse the overtures' movement of action: at the end of each film protagonists leave civilization and return to the wilderness (albeit with different intentions). Not only are these structural similarities found in films seventeen years apart, but their basic ambivalence toward the wilderness and civilization is present in each film's ending. Both films end with separation and unity, with those who return to the bosom of civilization and those who continue to wander in the wilderness. In each, the mediating value of the frontier is espoused, and yet that frontier remains an elusive phantom. While the structural endings of both films are similar, there is an essential difference that measures Ford's changed attitudes: in *Stagecoach* his hero and heroine go into the wilderness to begin something new, whereas in *The Searchers* his hero will vanish in the wilderness with no hope of a frontier rebirth. The music of the beginnings and the endings confirms this change. *Stagecoach* is a film with a continual forward thrust, whereas *The Searchers* projects stasis through its more oscillating, cyclical structure. In *The Searchers* the two musical themes of the beginning are repeated at the end (though the "Martha theme" has by then become associated with Debbie), while in *Stagecoach* the primary musical themes of the film (wilderness, savage, civilization, and journey) have been replaced by and subsumed in the "Ringo-Dallas theme."

Ford always structured his films around definitive midpoints. They are the fulcrums for the symmetry of his beginnings and endings, alternating sequential rhythms, and carefully balanced narrative aspects. The birth of the child in *Stagecoach* is the axis of the film's every ingredient. It occurs in the middle of the film's running time. It is the mythic event of the narrative's mythic discourse, bringing Ringo and Dallas together so Ringo can both give up his vengeance quest and complete it. It also unifies the passengers so they are able to withstand their final ordeal in the wilderness. *Stagecoach* has a central body consisting of three way station stops and the journeys between. The birth sequence is solidly situated in the middle stop, which is both the most narratively significant and the longest. With an average 12.4-second shot length (almost three seconds longer than the two surrounding sequences) there is a sense of cinematographic stability at the film's center. Finally, two new musical themes are introduced during this sequence: the "infant theme" and the "Ringo-Dallas theme." Dallas and Ringo become joined through the infant, and this unification becomes the metaphor for the entire journey.

The Searchers also has a definitive midpoint. But in this film it is not a mythic event (which says a good deal about Ford's changed approach to myth); instead, Ford developed his axis around a narratively complex set of events. Lorrie (Vera Miles) reads Martin's (Jeffrey Hunter) letter to her parents and her suitor. In it Martin tells of Ethan (John

TABLE 1
Stagecoach: Narrative Structure

Sequence no.	1	2	3	4	5
ACTION	boarding the stage	1st leg of journey	1st stop (noon meal)	2d leg of journey	2d stop (night)
SETTING	desert; Tonto/ town	stage; desert	frontier way station	stage; desert	frontier way station
FUNCTION	overture establishes journey (ordeal) form; introduces vengeance theme	exposition; establishes vengeance theme; movement	societal conflict; stasis	exposition; movement	prelude to mythic event; stasis
MYTHIC DISCOURSE	failure of civilization	initiates ordeal in wilderness	failure of democracy	conflicts and alliances established	societal breakdown
MUSIC	mythic themes introduced: wilderness; savage (Indian); civilization (honky-tonk); journey	journey; wilderness	Mrs. Mallory; Dallas	journey; wilderness	Mexican; Mrs. Mallory
PUNCTUATION					
Min. & sec.	13:37	8:17	9:56	6:43	7:34
No. of shots	89	66	62	41	49
Avg. length of shot	9.2 sec.	7.5 sec.	9.6 sec.	9.8 sec.	9.3 sec.
Intrascenic transitions	3 scenes; 3 dissolves	3 scenes; 3 dissolves	2 scenes; 1 dissolve	1 scene	2 scenes; 1 dissolve
Interscenic transitions	1 dissolve	fade	fade	fade	fade

6	7	8	9	10	11	12
the birth	morning departure	3d leg of journey	3d stop (river crossing)	Indian attack	final stop (destination)	departure and return
station interior	frontier way station	stage; desert	ferry; river	stage; desert	Lordsburg/ town	edge of town
midpoint: mythic event;	exposition; stasis and movement	exposition; movement	prelude: test before final ordeal	climax: ordeal	climax: quest (vengeance)	coda
unity and redemption	hero willing to give up vengeance; denied	hero and sage mediate	expiation: fire and water	completion of ordeal in the wilderness	completion of vengeance quest	unity and separation
infant; Ringo-Dallas	journey; savage	wilderness; savage	savage; wilderness	wilderness; savage; Mrs. Mallory; cavalry	civilization; Ringo-Dallas	Ringo-Dallas
6:12	10:36	2:14	2:40	8:55	15:13	2:21
30	65	14	16	106	100	6
12.4 sec.	9.8 sec.	9.6 sec.	11.3 sec.	5.0 sec.	9.1 sec.	23.5 sec.
1 scene	2 scenes	1 scene	2 scenes; 1 dissolve	1 scene	1 scene	1 scene

fade   4 dissolves   3 dissolves   2 dissolves   2 dissolves   1 cut

TABLE 2
The Searchers: Narrative Structure

Sequence no.	1	2	3	4
ACTION	Ethan's return	Scar's raid	1st search	1st return
SETTING	desert; brother's home	desert; brother's home	desert	Jorgensen's place
FUNCTION	overture; psychological exposition and motivation	narrative trigger: vengeance and search themes established	search and failure; movement	new incentive; conflict; stasis
MYTHIC DISCOURSE	wilderness: prodigal returns: sibling conflict; repressed love	wilderness: realization of nightmare; savagery	failure of civilization: renunciation and vengeance	Dioscuric mediator (Martin): conflict, civilization or wilderness
MUSIC	searchers theme; Martha theme	Scar; wilderness danger; tragic Martha	silence; scar	silence; Lorrie
PUNCTUATION:				
Min. & sec.	12:30	9:00	16:50	10:10
No. of shots	67	61	125	57
Avg. length of shot	11.2 sec.	8.9 sec.	8.1 sec.	10.7 sec.
Intrascenic transitions	5 scenes; 4 dissolves	3 scenes; 1 fade; 1 dissolve	9 scenes; 8 dissolves	3 scenes; 2 dissolves
Interscenic transitions	3 dissolves; in desert	3 dissolves; the burial	4 dissolves; search through seasons	1 dissolve

5	6	7	8	9
The letter: 2d search	3d search	2d return	final search	final return
trading post; campsite; Jorgensen's; Indian camp; winter plains; cavalry fort	Southwest Territory; Scar's camp; desert; cave	Jorgensen's	desert; Scar's camp	Jorgensen's; desert
episodic midpoint; exposition; search; movement and stasis; conflict	materialization of search; failure; conflict; movement	prelude: new incentive; stasis	climax: search and vengeance	coda
conflict: cultural, racial, and personal	civilization or savagery: Ethan confronts his double (Scar)	Dioscuric mediator (Martin): conflict; final search	success: savagery and civilization = frontier	homecoming: civilization & wanderer; unity & separation
wilderness danger; Look; cavalry; Charlie song: "Gone Again, Skip to My Lou"	Scar; Martha (now Debbie); wilderness danger	"Shall We Gather at the River"; "Yellow Rose of Texas"	wilderness danger; Scar; Martha/Debbie	Martha/Debbie; searchers
23:16	14:27	15:43	8:52	1:50
128	98	53	54	8
10.9 sec.	8.8 sec.	17.8 sec.	9.8 sec.	13.8 sec.
3 scenes, and 4 scenes within letter-reading sequence; 5 dissolves	3 scenes; 2 dissolves	3 scenes; 1 dissolve	3 scenes; 2 dissolves	1 dissolve
	2 dissolves: ride through burning sun	1 dissolve	1 dissolve	1 dissolve

Wayne) and his longest journey in search of Debbie (Natalie Wood). Virtually all the film's conflicts and themes are woven through this sequence. Seven scenes alternate between Lorrie's angry reading and Martin's and Ethan's frustrated searching. An important clue is discovered; tension increases between Martin and Ethan; the romance between Lorrie and Martin begins to fade; cultural and social tensions rise to the surface: the seasons change. Shifts in narrative style, length of running time, and tone set this middle sequence apart. This sequence has three different narrative voices (unusual in a Ford film): Lorrie's letter reading; Martin's narration of events; and characters' dialogue. At 23 minutes, 16 seconds, this sequence is more than six minutes longer than any of the others. Finally, for such a central episode in an essentially tragic film the tone is surprisingly comic. From *Stagecoach* to *The Searchers* Ford changed his method of presenting narrative midpoints, but not their essential function. In both films they are the unifying conduits through which the elements of the first halves are channeled, then released as denouement, climax, and coda.

The final major structural principal to which Ford adhered throughout his career was that of alternating sequences. Both *Stagecoach* and *The Searchers* are based on alternating sequences of movement and stasis. Because *Stagecoach* is a linear journey film, it juxtaposes traveling and stopping, while *The Searchers*, an oscillating quest film, alternates search and return. These alternating rhythms produce the effects of energy, change, and respite from the tyranny of symmetrical order. Ford had honed the essential characteristic of classical narrative technique into a filmic high art: the perfect balance between order and variety.

Table 3 identifies those narrative aspects that could shed light on these two films' narrative methods. The table lists each narrative aspect, then, on a horizontal plane, identifies each film's characteristic. Thus it is possible to compare quickly, say, the form of *Stagecoach* and *The Searchers*. The cumulative effect of such listings and comparisons should produce a number of conclusions about the narrative methods of Ford and his screenwriters. (To guide the reader from expository prose to the table, I have parenthetically inserted in the text each narrative aspect's table number whenever I make reference to it.)

Though differences do exist between these two films, those narrative aspects pertaining to romance are numerous and similar. The narrative form (1) of both films takes the essential quest-adventure form of romance. While the ostensible quests are for vengeance, they lead to the ultimate goal of the searchers, which is to discover their identities. Northrop Frye believes that, in ritual terms, "the quest-romance is the victory of fertility over the waste land."[2] In Westerns the metaphor of the wasteland operates on many levels. Certainly it is the vast, empty setting (17, 18). The desert Southwest, that wilderness no-man's-land, is the physical setting which acts as the indexical signifier for the wilderness self of the quest hero. Seeking and accomplishing vengeance, which two of the heroes (Ringo and Ethan) do, is not a victory over the wasteland. But Ringo finds love and turns his life toward the fertile, new beginnings of family and home and land. In *The Searchers* the victory over the wasteland is complicated by the twin heroes (10) one of whom, Martin Pawley (Jeffrey Hunter), is the youthful romance quester. Like Ringo, Martin rejects vengeance but must carry the quest through to its conclusion. Both settle down after the quest, secure in their identities. The other hero, Ethan, is the aging hero who must live out his life in the wasteland. Though he is too old to be fully redeemed, by not killing his niece he is partially redeemed. This choice represents his small victory over the wasteland because it allows him to deny and reject his deepest savage self. Thus all three heroes from the two films can claim to have been humanized by their quests. Frye states that the form of romance is dialectical in nature.[3] This fits the qualities of these two romances whose mediating heroes (10) are poised between both the positive and the negative aspects of each side of the major polarity, wilderness and civilization. For instance, the wasteland in these films is not simply associated with the wilderness. Both civilization and the wilderness are capable of engendering wastelands over which there must be victories. The romance must be sequential or processional,[4] and so these two films are, having cause and effect mechanisms (7), chronological or logical syntaxes (8), and linear and oscillating movement (2). Romance also has a strong cyclical quality[5] which is found in these films' narrative rhythms (3) of movement and stasis and in their symmetry (4). Both films have patterns that imply movement toward an end that on closer inspection begins to look more like the beginning, an ending that leads to movement toward a new beginning. The suggestion in both films is that these are never-ending cycles in the progression of its mythic mode (6), American civilization.

Other overriding conclusions can be drawn from these charts. First, basic similarities between the two films reinforce the view that there was an essential continuity in Ford's career. Second, *The Searchers* is a more psychologically complex film. There has been a shift in the Fordian hero from a public man able to respond to strangers and society without having to authenticate his inner being to the private man whose every gesture and response are manifestations of his inner self. Will Rogers, Ringo, Abe Lincoln, Gil Martin, Tom Joad, and even Wyatt Earp were readily absorbed into their public roles. Their psyches were not on public display. And while they all had private moments of personal emotion on-screen, these incidents never affected their public persona.

Beginning with Lieutenant Colonel Owen Thursday (Henry Fonda)

TABLE 3

Aspects of Narrative	*Stagecoach*	*The Searchers*
1 form	journey (passengers); quest (Ringo)	quest
2 movement	linear (Tonto to Lordsburg)	oscillating (search and return)
3 narrative rhythm	movement and stasis	movement and stasis
4 symmetry	moderate	strong
5 generic mode	vengeance Western (Romance)	vengeance Western (Romance)
6 mythic mode	myth of American civilization (journey/quest-ordeal)	myth of American civilization (quest-ordeal)
7 mechanism	cause and effect	cause and effect
8 syntax	chronological	logical
9 expression	moderately complex	complex
10 function of hero(es)	mediator	dioscuric mediators
11 characterization	folk archetypes	psychological beings and cultural representatives
12 character motivation	moderate (societal, situational)	strong (psychological)
13 music	American folk tunes	original character themes
14 music placement	related to character or place; prominently used in sequence transitions	related to character or place; prominently used in sequence transitions
15 coloration	black and white	Technicolor
16 space (movement)	unified, limited, controlled	varied, unlimited, subject to moving goal

TABLE 3—*Continued*

Aspects of Narrative	*Stagecoach*	*The Searchers*
17 space (setting)	exterior-interior: wilderness, way stations, frontier towns, stagecoach	exterior-interior: wilderness, homes, way stations, campsites, Indian camps
18 space (scale)	contained	vast
19 running time	97 minutes	119 minutes
20 fictive time	2 days	5 years
21 temporal unity	unified, compressed	elliptical, elongated
22 punctuation	fades: 5; dissolves: 18; shots: 636	fades: 1; dissolves: 41; shots: 675
23 segmentation	shorter sequences: 12 in 97 min.; varied scenic structure: 1) short scenes set off by dissolves; 2) average length scenes set off by dissolves; 3) long scenes that rely on parallel syntagmas to encompass the actions of a relatively large group	longer sequences: 9 in 119 min.; unified scenic structure: 1) all scenes (with the exception of the preparation for the massacre and Marty's letter to Lorrie sequence) are essentially autonomous segments relying on descriptive syntagmas set off by dissolves
24 avg. shots per min.	6.6	5.7
25 avg. length of shot	9.1 sec.	10.6 sec.
26 framing	rigidly composed; traditional use of reaction shot/reverse angle shot, offscreen space	more naturally composed; a good deal of untraditional use of offscreen space
27 depth of field	moderately deep	deeper, more expressively effective

TABLE 3—*Continued*

Aspects of Narrative	Stagecoach	The Searchers
28 camera distance	1) more close-ups; 2) more medium close-ups; 3) more medium shots; 4) more deliberate establishing shots	1) few close-ups; 2) more medium long shots, 3) more non-establishing long shots
29 camera angles	1) diagonals; 2) sparing use of high and low angle shots	1) diagonals; 2) sparing use of high and low angle shots

in *Fort Apache* the cracks begin to show. Ford became interested in more visibly complex psychological characterization. We begin to see the complete persona break through the social self. In *She Wore a Yellow Ribbon* Nathan Brittles (John Wayne) sniffles with emotion in public when he is presented with a watch; in *Rio Grande* Kirby Yorke's (John Wayne) family problems are played out in front of the men he commands. To achieve this greater psychological realism Ford, to a degree, changed his style.

Using narrative aspects as reference points, it is possible to identify those elements Ford retained from his earlier period as well as those he changed, at least within the Western genre.

The similarities between *Stagecoach* and *The Searchers* are these: (3) narrative rhythm; (5) generic mode; (6) mythic mode; (7) narrative mechanism; (10) function of hero(s); (14) placement of music; (17) spatial setting; (29) camera angles. On the basis of these likenesses it is possible to say that Ford continued to make vengeance romances about the myth of American civilization with mediating heroes at the center of narratives that were driven forward by casual mechanisms. Ford refused to budge from a narrative rhythm of movement and stasis, a counterpointed use of silence and music with the music thematically tied to character and setting, and a strict adherence to diagonal placement of the camera on the horizontal plane and a limited middle range with respect to high and low angles on the vertical plane. In other words, Ford remained a traditionally narrative romancer and myth-maker and a classical stylist.

In *The Searchers* Ethan is a far more psychologically motivated (12) force than Ringo in *Stagecoach*. He is obsessively driven by quest rather than journey considerations. Whereas Ringo is willing to forego his vengeance quest, Ethan is the compelled questor who will allow nothing to stand in the way of his irrational mission, his pathological quirk. The heroes of the late films are nihilists, escapists, or wild dreamers: Colonel Thursday in *Fort Apache*, Sean Thornton (John Wayne) in *The Quiet Man*, Spig Wead (John Wayne) in *The Wings of Eagles*, Tom Doniphon and Liberty Valance, "Guns" Donovan (John Wayne) and "Boats" Gilhooley (Lee Marvin) in *Donovan's Reef*, and Miss Andrews (Margaret Leighton) in *7 Women*.

In these late films the hero has become the "hero," still a larger-than-life individualist, but now one who is enough out of touch with social reality that he or she cannot fill the role of public hero. Their heroic qualities are now open to question, which is one of the reasons these films often failed at the box office. Ford and his primary screenwriter of this period, Frank Nugent, tried to compensate for this hero manqúe by creating another more socially integrated figure. Thus, these films usually have dual heroes whose mythic function is that of twin or dioscuric mediators: John Wayne and Maureen O'Hara in a number of films; Fonda and Wayne in *Fort Apache*; O'Hara and Tyrone Power in *The Long Gray Line*; Spencer Tracy and Jeffrey Hunter in *The Last Hurrah*; Wayne and William Holden in *The Horse Soldiers*; Hunter and Woody Strode in *Sergeant Rutledge*; Jimmy Stewart and Richard Widmark in *Two Rode Together*; Stewart and Wayne in *Liberty Valance*; Lee Marvin and Wayne in *Donovan's Reef*; and finally, Anne Bancroft and Margaret Leighton in *7 Women*. In *The Searchers*, of course, it is Martin Pawley, "he who follows," who shadows Ethan in order to protect Ethan from himself. Martin is the sane part-Cherokee accepted by white society, while Ethan is the obsessed white man more in tune with the Indian, Scar (Henry Brandon). Ethan's overt quest is to wreak vengeance on the murdering rapists of his beloved sister-in-law. Martin knows that if Ethan succeeds, Ethan will lose his standing within human society.

With a psychological complexity never before equalled in Ford's earlier films, Ethan's quest can be seen as a madness triggered by guilt and self-hatred. The opening sequence of *The Searchers*, for instance, is filmed in such a way that the viewer can speculate, without distorting the text, that Ethan's obsession is the result of his failure to marry Martha. Thus, his secret lust (psychological) is wedded to his wilderness self (mythical). He sets off to destroy Scar, not simply for the sake of societal justice and natural law (mythical), but to eradicate his savage alter ego (psychological). Ethan hates Scar because he hates himself; he must kill Scar to exorcise the guilt he himself bears. For, unconsciously, Ethan wished to commit Scar's crimes, killing his brother and raping his sister-in-law. Scar, as the name suggests, is Ethan's mark of Cain, his manqué. With Ethan's psychologically unconscious dimension established early in the film, his inability to destroy Debbie, his spiritual daughter, at the end of the film is a consistent psychological reaction. As he raises the grown Debbie into the air, an unconscious association links that action with the time he raised her as a young girl, in the beginning of the film. Finally, Ford, by having the "Martha theme" played during Ethan's lifting of the adult Debbie, has further reinforced the psychological validity of Ethan's refusal to kill the tainted girl. She is both the child he played with and the woman he loved. To kill her would be to go over the edge. Ford's heroes, no matter how flawed they are, never go that far. By scalping Scar, Ethan has teetered on the brink of the savage abyss, but a woman has returned him to life, just as he returns her to civilization (white civilization, that is). Ethan would surely have destroyed himself had he destroyed Debbie. As it is, civilization simply shuts him out, condemning him to wander forever between the winds. The symmetry (4) of this film is not just visual and archetypal, but also psychological, thus far more complex and powerful than *Stagecoach*.

The force of the quest in *The Searchers* determines its movement (2) and syntax (8). *Stagecoach*'s journey form drove the narrative in a straight line. The stage has a route from Tonto to Lordsburg. It is this journey form (1) that largely determines the narrative's sequential order (8), spatial elements (16, 17, 18), fictive time (20), and temporal unity (21). The movement is linear (2) because the route is undirectionally established; the time it takes to reach Lordsburg (20) is controlled by the distance and the forces of interruption. The spatial elements of *Stagecoach* are also controlled by the journey format. The predictable rhythm of traveling and resting establishes a unity of movement (16) and setting (17). The journey's preestablished pattern of linear movement and chronological temporal order determines the film's syntax (8). Ringo's quest, which could have led the film into an entirely different spatial and temporal direction, is subsumed by the journey. The journey is a public event, which means that Ringo, by subordinating his quest, is able to remain a societally integrated hero. On the stage journey none of the relationships are deeply psychological, no one's motive for traveling is obsessive.

On the other hand, the more psychologically powerful quest form of *The Searchers* places the film's spatial and temporal direction on the actions of the hunter (Ethan) and the hunted (Scar). There can be no preestablished pattern. The fictive time (20) will continue as long as Ethan is willing to chase Scar, and the spatial setting and movement (16, 17) will continue to change as long as Scar is willing to run. The structure, then, is based on the fact that Ethan is a "critter who'll just keep coming on" and that Scar is a Nawyaki Comanche whose tribal name means, "sorta like round about. Man says he's goin' one place, means to go a-t'other." Ford joins the psychological dimension to the mythical by suggesting that Ethan's search has taken him to the ends of the earth, through the seasons, and for an eternity. In this way Ethan's psychological search becomes transformed into the wilderness hero's quest. The syntax of *The Searchers* (8), therefore, is determined by the logic of Ethan's psyche, that of obsessed hunter and wilderness quester. Its elliptical and elongated temporal scheme (20, 21) has the achronology of both mythic and subjective time, further reinforcing the film's dualistic approach, the psychological and mythical.

Supporting these changes in the characterization of Ford's protagonists was a new approach toward his supporting casts (11). *Stagecoach's* passengers were easily identifiable folk types, bordering on clichéd stereotypes. This was in keeping with Ford's emphasis on public personae. These characters were to be deeply rooted in generic conventions, popular culture, and folk tales. What little complexity they have is derived from their dual roles as contrasting folk types (character interaction) and changed individuals (surviving the mythical ordeal in the wilderness). Ford was seldom satisfied with an unchanging, one-dimensional character type. Peacock, for instance, might have been no more than a comic weakling. Instead, Ford endowed him with the visual characteristics of a preacher and the personality of a jellyfish. Peacock is given the anomalous profession of whiskey drummer. All this, combined with his transformation, gives Peacock dimension. Dallas is more than just the prostitute-with-the-heart-of-gold; she is also the mythic mother. Mrs. Mallory is more than just an upper-crust snob; she is also a woman who is determined to find her husband regardless of the danger. Each character produces ambivalent reactions in the viewer, and this generates a certain complexity. Ford was sharp in his casting and shrewd in his directing of secondary characters. No character served as mere window dressing. They enhanced the world of each film by reflecting aspects of the hero's personality, by filling out a community with credible human beings, by providing the tensions and crosscurrents in dialectical issues, and by creating the comic counterpointing so crucial to Ford's aesthetic.

By the time of *The Searchers* these folk types had basically disappeared. This does not mean that Ford's secondary characters became so fully human that they vied with the protagonists for psychological dimension. It is simply more difficult to give each character a folk label. They are blessed with more disturbingly ambivalent personalities. Sam Clayton (Ward Bond) switches from Reverend to Captain of the Texas Rangers with dazzling speed and unsettling ease. Mose Harper (Hank Worden) as the most mentally disturbed of Ford's idiot savants, is both in touch with the cosmic vibrations and earthbound enough to know he needs only a "roof over Old Mose's head and a rocking chair by the fire." "Old Mose knows." And so he does. The psychic reserves these characters display typifies Ford's later approach to characterization. Their private selves are revealed again and again: Reverend/Captain Clayton looking away in discrete embarrassment, while Martha strokes Ethan's coat; Lorrie's frustrated sexuality rising to the surface; Lars Jorgensen's (John Qualen) unabashed pride in his wife's learning; Charlie McCorry's (Ken Curtis) switch from simpleton to poetic balladeer.

Ford had to make some stylistic changes in order to achieve this greater psychological realism, all the while conveying the mythic properties of the narrative. By 1956 any use of black and white would have been a stylization (15). The American neorealists of the 1950s were filming in black and white either because they could more effectively make statements about their bleak visions of society and/or because they had limited budgets. Ford needed color in *The Searchers* to convey unobtrusive reality, stylized nightmare violence, and mythic vastness. Color enhanced the scale (18) and range of Monument Valley's mythic setting.

Ford's films became consistently longer (19) after the war, as though he needed more time to present adequately his more complex characters. But, above all, he began to pull his camera back (28), use longer takes (27, 25), and give greater spatial unity to each scene (23). His growing interest in realism coincided with his continued reliance on mise-en-scène and depth-of-field photography. André Bazin argued that the realism in Jean Renoir's films, for instance, was the result of the primacy of mise-en-scène over montage: Renoir "forced himself to look back beyond the resources provided by montage and so uncovered the secret of a film form that would permit everything to be said without chopping the world up into little fragments, that would reveal the hidden meanings in people and things without disturbing the unity natural to them."[6] Ford understood this principle long before it became a critical commonplace.

In *The Searchers* Ford's elimination of fade-outs in favor of dissolves reinstills an almost poetic unity and fluid plasticity to the film. Where *Stagecoach* employs fade-outs, *The Searchers* substitutes brief transitional units composed of three or four dissolves in quick succession. Yet Ford retained one stylistic principle from both periods: as each film moves toward its denouement and climax, the major transitional devices dividing sequences, fade-outs, and multiple dissolves, are almost completely abandoned in favor of the one quick dissolve that gives the impression of an almost uninterrupted rush toward the climax.

Nick Browne has argued persuasively that the noon-meal scene in *Stagecoach* has a complex point-of-view structure. Ford used subjective camera perspectives in other sequences as well: the dolly-in introduction of Ringo, the flying-in-the-dirt shoot-out, and Dallas's

Ethan (John Wayne) envisions the massacre in the desert, in The Searchers.

movement toward the camera/Ringo after the shoot-out. Later in his career Ford rejected these point-of-view techniques as obtrusive and simplistic. As his films became more psychologically complex, a more subtle and integrated method was needed to express the inner states of a character's consciousness.

Ford solved this dilemma by developing a number of almost realistic dream states. This was most effectively used in *The Quiet Man* where virtually the entire film (from the moment the cart passes under the train) is the playing out of Sean Thornton's (John Wayne) dream of returning to Ireland. In *The Searchers* this process occurs once during the massacre and again during Lorrie's reading of Martin's letter. In the first instance, the Rangers have been drawn out away from the ranches by a decoy. Ethan finally realizes that an Indian murder raid is inevitable. The Rangers ride back to the ranchers, with the exception of Ethan and Mose who stay behind to rest and feed their horses. As Ethan begins to wipe the lather off his horse, the camera holds— not in a close-up—on his deeply introverted eyes and his powerfully tragic expression. Then it cuts—it does not dissolve as it has in *every other* scene change in the film—to Aaron's family discovering and preparing for the raid. The sunset is a stylized soundstage red. Only these two seemingly minor indicators point to this incident as a product of

Ethan's consciousness, his nightmare. Then it stops short just before
the murder and rape, as when one awakens from a nightmare just before the actual violence. This ending is punctuated by the only fade-
out in the film, as though it is Ethan's nightmare that fades.

Later in the film Charlie McCorry delivers to Lorrie a long letter
from Martin. Her reading of the letter and the depiction of its contents
constitute the film's longest scene within the longest sequence. As with
Ethan's nightmare incident, this scene is edited on the basis of cuts
rather than dissolves. Since great spatial and temporal leaps are made
during this scene, one would have expected dissolves to be the transitional punctuation. Instead, there is one continuous flow of action
between Lorrie's reading and Martin's tribulations with a squaw named
Look whom he inadvertently buys. Much of this scene is comic, often
distastefully and racistly so. Is there an explanation for this? Ford was
usually extremely careful to portray Indians with dignity and a mini-
mum of racial stereotyping. The structure of the scene, with no dissolves or flashback techniques, indicates that Lorrie's consciousness is
rendering the action. When we are first taken back to Ethan's and
Martin's action, there is no synchronic sound. Instead, Lorrie's diachronic voice-over continues her presence on into the now-actual
events of the searchers. If these images are hers, then Ford's dream
techniques might explain the low comedy and racial stereotyping of
these actions. After all, white, young, and in love, Lorrie is outraged
by the letter's "how I got me a squaw" contents. Martin's words supply
only the bare outline of the story; Lorrie's vivid and subjective imagination fills in what we see. By the end of the film her racist attitudes
become explicit. She tries for the last time to prevent Martin from
following Ethan, by agreeing with Ethan that Debbie should have a
bullet in her brain for having lived among the Indians. This is the kind
of dangerous, complex, and open form of narrative expression Ford
used in his later years.

7

The Dream, the Myths, and Jeffersonianism

THE AMERICAN DREAM is a powerful stimulant in American culture. Some believe that no country on earth has its national destiny expressed in such sweepingly forward-looking terms. Since this concept of destiny has been called the dream, the implications are that it is not quite real, that it is deeply embedded in our national unconscious, that it is an ideal for the future, that it is symbol-laden, and that it is ephemeral. It is a multifaceted dream because millions of people from different lands and eras have dreamt it and shaped it. It has been given definition by the expectations of those who have arrived on our shores for the first time and of those who have participated in it. Those expectations have been: the right to the pursuit of happiness; a democratic nation where all people are created equal; an abundance of land that any person may and should acquire; a New World ·where every person could be a pioneer on a frontier; and a righteous empire that should civilize the wilderness through constant westward expansion. Because of these expectations Americans are free, innocent individualists who keep moving and changing in search of new frontiers. And that search keeps the nation strong, self-sufficient, and progressive. This is the dream, and since it is so unerringly positive in outlook, it has contributed to what many observers have felt to be America's unflagging optimism.

Since this dream is America's Holy Grail, many stories have been told about the quest for it, and since the dream is so positive and unattainable, many of them exist solely to reconcile the dream with the inevitable reality. These stories are the mythic tales of the American dream. But the dream is so vast that each tale must focus on only a few mythic themes. In a certain number of films directed by John Ford I have identified six mythic themes of the American dream. I believe these to be essential myths of that dream. One crucial myth, however, is missing from Ford's vision, the myth of the pursuit of happiness. Ford's generally serious, tragic, and moral sensibilities drove him away from this theme. This myth does, however, surface in a number of his films, particularly in such comedies as *Donovan's Reef*; and Hollywood certainly suffered from no dearth of pursuit-of-happiness films from other hands.

Ford as mythmaker and filmic storyteller of basic American myths chose or had chosen for him original stories with mythical potential. From there he and his screenwriters deepened and sharpened these works' mythic focus. This meant they had to deepen the gulf between the polarities of any thematic tension, while elevating the rhetorical qualities of each pole. For instance, a story about ranchers and villagers would be transformed into a tale of the wilderness and civilization. And by adding a cowboy who both mediates the quarrel and searches for his own identity and goal the screenwriters could raise their character to the mythic level of quest hero who is responsible for resolving the dilemmas posed by the division and the quest. American mythic themes, therefore, are defined by the problems, contradictions, and paradoxes that have been raised during someone's quest for some version of the American dream. The dream could not exist without the myths because it would be both too good to be true and too cruel in its failed expectations. Since the myths expose the dangers of the dream, the dream is then able to survive as both a reality and an ideal. This is the method and function of mythology and it is the method and function of Ford's romances.

Each myth presents dilemmas for its heroes, and it is through a successful mediation or resolution of these problems that the heroes are transported into the mythic realm. Though each myth is named after its positive dream quality, all mythic heroes and qualities carry both positive and negative values. Thus, the American Adam is not solely innocent; the American frontier is not eternal and does not symbolize freedom alone; American agrarianism has destroyed the land, is inefficient, and leads to isolation; the American democrat may be authoritarian, while equality in an American democracy may be only a dream to some; American individualism can undermine community solidarity; and American civilization has destroyed the wilderness, exploited Native Americans, and led to overcivilization. These tensions, finally, must settle into the deepest issue, that of whether myths and mythic heroes are a positive or negative force in society and culture. This question is best expressed in this exchange of dialogue from Bertolt Brecht's play *Galileo:* "Pity the land that breeds no hero." "No, pity the land that needs a hero." Ford and Brecht ultimately disagreed when forced to choose between the two. Ford believed in the first statement, Brecht in the second. Yet Ford's films do show the destructive, as well as constructive, value of heroes and myths. None of his films details this dilemma more clearly than *Fort Apache*.

In the three Will Rogers films the American Adam is at times overwhelmed by the forces of civilization that have invaded Eden. There is progression from the Edenic *Steamboat Round the Bend*, which is too static, timeless, and comfortable to encompass the energetic forward motion that is part of the American vision of Eden. Judge Priest's world, however, is an acceptable Eden. Here the dangers of civilization, inequality, corruption, loneliness, tragedy, and restriction haunt this heroic mediator. Still, he resolves the conflicts without making a legal judgment. The judge and his friends sweep them away in a tidal wave of community spirit. In the contemporary setting of 1930s New England is Eden, after the Fall, as civilization in *Dr. Bull* is rampant. The mythic mediator, who accomplishes some good under severe restrictions, is dismissed from his official town post. He is the Last Adam, thrown out of a desecrated Eden. Adam's innocence and isolation make him ineffective in the face of civilization—that is, his Adamic qualities actually enhance the very process he fights. Irony resides in these myths, thereby allowing them to remain modern.

While the myth of the American frontier suggests an eternal place, any literal frontier ends somewhere, sometime. What is eternal about frontiers is their cyclical resilience. Somehow there will always be a new frontier—somewhere. And though freedom is coveted on the frontier, people are trapped between the violence of the wilderness and the corruption of American ideals by the forces of civilization. Ford's frontier films demonstrate this dilemma in different ways on different frontiers. Those who are innocent must kill to survive (Lana in *Drums along the Mohawk*; Ringo in *Stagecoach*), while others must expose their innocence to the frivolous elements of civilization (young Abe Lincoln). Each frontier is a hard, violent, exploitative place that will cease to exist, which means that its inhabitants must either move to an equally tempestuous frontier or stay put and become civilized. Each frontier film's conclusion, though it seems to have resolved the immediate problems, always suggests that more tough times are yet to come. The Western cliché of riding into the sunset is, therefore, double-edged. The flag raising at the end of *Drums along the Mohawk* reminds us of the wars and troubles still to face this new nation, and the storm in the off-screen distance of *Young Mr. Lincoln* conveys the trials Lincoln and the nation have yet to encounter.

Though I have not devoted a separate chapter to the myth of the American democrat, this myth pervades all of Ford's American romances. Certain films, however, are specifically concerned with the threats that may endanger a democracy: the incipient fascism in *Young Mr. Lincoln* and the fascism that when coupled with racism becomes an explosive force in *The Sun Shines Bright*. Other films explore the problems of racial inequality within a democracy (*Sergeant Rutledge*, *Two Rode Together*, and *Cheyenne Autumn*). Many of Ford's films present a dilemma peculiar to American myths: how do mythic heroes, who are by definition superior to other humans, retain their democratic qualities? Ford's solution was to place these heroes against a vast array of snobs. The manifest irony of the situation resolves the apparent contradiction: while snobs believe themselves to be better human beings, they aren't, whereas democratic heroes don't believe themselves to be better, and they are, but only in the sense that they have the skills, talents, and fortitude to defend, communicate, and mediate for a community. In this way the American democrat remains an equal human being who just happens to have qualities that are important for the society.

The latent essence of the myth of American agrarianism is that civilization has destroyed the land. The irony of the myth is that the agrarian ideal, benignly pastoral though it may have seemed, really began the civilizing process that eventually destroyed that ideal. Within the American dream the agrarian ideal came into conflict with the entrepreneurial ideal. And since the two most powerful of Ford's agrarian films basically had contemporary settings, they are about the failure of agrarianism and the victory of entreprenurialism in America. The more despairing film, *Tobacco Road*, lacks a mythic hero, while in *The Grapes of Wrath* the hero redirects his search away from the agrarian ideal.

In Ford's films of the myth of American individualism supremely individualistic mythic heroes are shown accommodating themselves to the restrictions of their community. Unchecked individualism has no place in Ford's world. But the irony of this myth is that the more an individualist becomes integrated into a community, the more lonely he becomes. Solitude is a state of being, while community is a duty. This supports both the dilemma and its resolution.

The myth of American civilization raises two basic questions: Is progress good? Does a society lose an essential part of itself when it separates itself from the wilderness? In Ford's civilization films the answers to both questions are both yes and no. In these answers lie the ambivalence that always haunts myths and makes them real.

These are the six myths of our or any time in America—with the possible exception that Ford's particular heroes and settings are tied more to the founding of the industrial age in America, whereas we now appear to be making the transition into the post industrial era. It is possible, therefore, that films depicting the end of the industrial age and the founding of the technological age will have greater meaning for today's audiences. Still, this is primarily a matter of setting. The dilemmas raised by new individualistic pioneers settling new frontiers and preparing new land for new stages of democratic civilizations will always be with us.

From the stories told on film by Ford many issues and problems concerning human and institutional values have been raised and settled. Out of these it is possible to detect an ideology—a set of values and beliefs achieved over a given length of time through an accumulation of individual choices and social, political, and economic forces. Since my work has been an auteuristic study of one director's films, I will identify the ideology of the fourteen John Ford American films discussed in detail. I believe, however, that these films are representative of his entire career and that the ideology I will identify is by extension that of all Ford's films. To label something or someone is always dangerous because the charge of reductionism is close behind. Still, the process of identifying an ideology carries with it the responsibility of naming that ideology. Ford's films do not evade large ideological issues, since they are so rooted in American history and myth. At the same time, they present problems because, first, they raise and support so many cultural and philosophical polarities and then they mediate them. Does this mean that Ford, through his films, believed in everything and therefore nothing? He and his films have after all, been described as both liberal and conservative. I believe Ford's films espouse Jeffersonian democracy. Viewed today, such an ideology contains Ford's more extreme contradictions, which I will call liberal romanticism and conservative humanism. I hope at this point that these labels come as no particular surprise, nor that they appear to be so broad as to be meaningless.

Just as Alexis de Tocqueville in his *Democracy in America* saw America as the laboratory of democracy, so Ford saw the American frontier. The events, places, and people in each film represented a testing ground for American democracy. Ford's films are romantic in spirit because they are utopian quests. They posit an ideal place of the imagination where quest heroes searching for an ideal encounter the conflicts of a society and resolve or mediate the most important of them. This frontier utopianism is what draws together the Western and science fiction. Both genres deal with the same dilemmas. Though one sets the problems in the past and the other projects them into the future, both are really concerned with the present and the immediate future. Since there are at present no inhabitable Western or outerspace frontiers, both are speaking to the problems found in psychological and societal frontiers rather than the actual frontiers of open space. Either literally or metaphorically, the dilemmas embodied in mythic wildernesses and civilizations will always be with us.

The principles of democracy as they have been passed down to us from the Enlightenment and the eras of revolution have usually been perceived as liberal and progressive. And Ford's films have preserved a liberal reading of liberty, equality, and fraternity. If one views the contest between Jeffersonianism and Hamiltonianism as a crucial debate in American democracy, then one can say that Ford's films side decisively with Jefferson. This has been most apparent in the agrarian films, but beyond them the spirit of Jefferson lives in all of Ford's American romances. Time and again these films depict situations in which authority resides in the consent of the governed, while power on the basis of birth, wealth, or contract, a Hamiltonian position, is ridiculed.

Ford's films often show, particularly in his war pictures, that the primary function of government is to protect liberty. In fact, for Ford, defending democratic liberty was the *only* reason to go to war. Hamilton, however, believed that the government's final duty was to protect property. Now one could argue that in the West the cavalry was actually protecting property under the guise of protecting liberty—and this could be successfully argued with respect to much of America's warring—but not in the way Ford's films present acts of war. He remained a committed Jeffersonian in this regard.

Ford's films deal with issues of equality, specifically problems of social and racial equality. His films take seriously the credo that "all men are created equal." Ford's favorite situations have been those in which outcasts are treated unequally by factions of "civilized" society. The problem of racial equality, however, is a more sensitive one. Ford has been criticized in some quarters for his failure to humanize and credibly depict blacks and Native Americans. These critics condemn his lack of non-white points of view, his mere inclusion of Stepin Fetchit's fawning "Uncle Tom" caricatures, and his acceptance without guilt (on the screen) of the many Indians who are killed by whites. My position is that Ford was neither a radical reformer nor a racist. While Ford believed in equal rights for *all* human beings, he was also making films the settings of which, both in time and place, often demanded a depiction of racist behavior. The films' ideologies, however, did not accept such behavior. Nevertheless, in the 1930s, 1940s, and through much of the 1950s it was extremely difficult to make commercial films that took an overtly sympathetic position with respect to other races. In the late 1950s and 1960s Ford did direct and produce (through his own production company) a number of films that actively confronted racial prejudice. And in his private life he was known for his acts of generosity toward oppressed races, in particular, the Native Americans in and around Monument Valley. The fact is that there are many quiet, affecting moments of interracial human warmth in Ford's films: private moments between, for instance, Will Rogers and Stepin Fetchit. Probably from today's perspective the worst one could rationally say of Ford's racial ideology is that he unthinkingly accepted institutional racism and that he did not at every moment oppose and refuse to depict racist behavior on-screen.

And finally, Ford's films are always about the sustaining, building of, and the pressures on communities and social units—in other words, fraternity. As a number of historians have noted, modern democracies attempt to reconcile individualism and collectivism. An ideal democracy depends not only on an individual's freedom of personality, but also on the social and political equality of all the members of social and political groups. Ford, as a Jeffersonian, depicted both the tensions and the reconciliations of such a society. These problems were not limited to his military films, which simply heightened the issues. Many of his films, for instance, depict the disintegration of the family as the central unit in a society in favor of larger social units (usually films with contemporary settings [*Grapes of Wrath*, for one]), while other films (usually Westerns) present families beginning to be the key unit of a society. Ford's liberalism rejects autocracy within these social units. For instance, in *How Green Was My Valley* it is the father's unbending demand for total control that drives his sons to find greater freedom on democratic frontiers. Other instances of autocracy are always punished in Ford's films.

Yet it is here that we can begin to delineate between Ford's liberalism and conservatism. His rejection of autocracy is liberal, yet his acceptance of authority is now often viewed as conservative. Still, this can be explained by his belief in Jeffersonian democracy, which acknowledges that though all men are created equal and should have equal rights of opportunity, this does not mean that all men are equal. Talents, skills, and force of personality may place certain people in positions of authority. In Ford's films authority, gained democratically and for the good of social unit or society at large, should be respected and obeyed. By today's liberal standards even this much authority is viewed with skepticism and is often considered conservative. The liberal attacks upon military chain of command are a good case in point.

The existence of mythic heroes and the inexorable power of mythic pastness throws into relief the conservative aspects of Ford's world. Mythic heroes seem to gain their power, often viewed as inordinate power, through mysterious, hence undemocratic, means. And the force of the past that myths generate, that sense that the possibility for change is limited, contributes to Ford's conservatism. Some observers of democracy have realized that Jeffersonian agrarianism reinforced a deep conservative strain in America. For instance, de Tocqueville believed that the wide distribution of property and the authority invested in majority rule would lead inevitably to a stability of the center that could be construed as essentially conservative. Conservatism is also associated with those values tied to the land. Ford's films depict this reverence for the eternal values, the old ways, and the authenticity of primitivism.

Ford's films express a deep ambivalence with respect to change and stability, past and future, freedom and restriction, individualism and community, wilderness and civilization. These tensions could not be resolved. Only mediation was acceptable, a mediation that was an uneasy alliance held together by the mythic hero. This ambivalence extended to Ford's liberal and conservative ideology. However, on some issues he had no such qualms. He always favored agrarianism over industrialism, equality over class, the West over the East, empiricism over legalism, and experience over knowledge. To this extent we may describe Ford's ideology as falling within the broad parameters of liberal Jeffersonian democracy.

When Jefferson took office as a Republican he immediately proclaimed, "We are all Republicans—we are all Federalists." This same mediating instinct lurks in Ford's films. Partisan politics rarely surface on-screen. Instead, John Ford seemed always to proclaim through his films of the American dream, "We are all democrats—we are all Americans."

Notes and References

Preface

1. John Caughie, ed., *Theories of Authorship: A Reader* (London, 1981), 3.
2. J. A. Place, *The Non-Western Films of John Ford* (Secaucus, N. J., 1979), 21.
3. Andrew Sinclair, *John Ford* (New York, 1979), 141.
4. Northrop Frye, *Anatomy of Criticism* (Princeton: Princeton University Press, 1957), 186.
5. Frank McConnell, *Storytelling and Mythmaking* (New York, 1979), 105.

Chapter One

1. Andrew Sarris, *The John Ford Movie Mystery* (Bloomington, Ind., 1975), 51.
2. R. W. B. Lewis, *The American Adam* (Chicago: University of Chicago Press, 1955), 9.
3. Leo Marx, *The Machine in the Garden* (New York: Oxford University Press, 1964), 3.
4. Ibid., 87.

Chapter Two

1. Quoted in Henry Nash Smith, *Virgin Land* (Cambridge: Harvard University Press, 1950), 250.
2. Walter Prescott Webb, *The Great Frontier* (Austin: University of Texas Press, 1964), 303.
3. Ibid., 8-13.
4. André Bazin, *What is Cinema? I* (Berkeley, 1967), 149.
5. Will Wright, *Sixguns and Society* (Berkeley: University of California Press, 1975), 15.
6. Frank Gruber, *The Pulp Jungle* in John G. Cawelti, *The Six-Gun Mystique* (Bowling Green, Ohio: Bowling Green University Popular Press, 1971), 34-35.

7.   Richard Slotkin, *Regeneration Through Violence* (Middletown, Conn.: Wesleyan University Press, 1973), 5.

8.   Editors of *Cahiers du Cinéma*, *Screen*, 13:3 (Autumn, 1972): 5-47.

9.   Ibid., 17-18.

10.   Ibid., 15.

11.   Peter Lehman, "An Absence Which Becomes a Legendary Presence," *Wide Angle* 2:4 (1978): 36-42.

12.   *Cahiers du Cinéma*, 37.

13.   Bill Nichols, "Style, Grammar, and the Movies," in *Movies and Methods*, ed. Bill Nichols (Berkeley: University of California Press, 1976), 619.

14.   Quoted in John E. O'Connor, "A Reaffirmation of American Ideals: *Drums Along the Mohawk*," in *American History/American Film*, ed. John E. O'Connor and Martin A. Jackson (New York: Ungar, 1979), 102.

15.   Ibid., 102-3.

16.   Dan Ford, *Pappy: The Life of John Ford* (Englewood Cliffs, N.J., 1979), 140.

17.   Quoted in Smith, *Virgin Land*, 253.

18.   Sarris, *Movie Mystery*, 89.

Chapter Three

1.   Smith, *Virgin Land*, 135.

2.   Henry Bamford Parkes, *The American Experience* (New York: A. A. Knopf, 1947), 41.

3.   Frye, *Anatomy of Criticism*, 189.

4.   Chester E. Eisinger, "Jeffersonian Agrarianism in *The Grapes of Wrath*," in *A Casebook on The Grapes of Wrath* (New York: Thomas V. Crowell Co., 1968), 149.

5.   Ford, *Pappy*, 143.

6.   Peter Bogdanovich, *John Ford* (Berkeley, 1978), 76.

7.   T. S. Eliot, "The Waste Land," *The Complete Poems and Plays* (New York: Harcourt, Brace & World, 1952), 38.

8.   See Marx, *The Machine in the Garden*, 19-23, and Smith, *Virgin Land*, 145-54.

9.   Robert D. Jacobs, "The Humor of Tobacco Road," *The Comic Imagination in American Literature*, ed. Louis D. Rubin (New Brunswick, N.J.: Rutgers University Press, 285-99.

10.   Ibid., 294.

11.   Frye, *Anatomy of Criticism*, 185.

12.   Sylvia Jenkins Cook, *From Tobacco Road to Route 66* (Chapel Hill: University of North Carolina Press, 1976), 161.

Chapter Four

1.   Franz Alexander, *Our Age of Unreason* (New York: J. B. Lippincott, 1942), 137.

2.   Ralph Waldo Emerson, "Self-Reliance," *Complete Essays and Other Writings* (New York: Random House, 1950), 169.

3. Henry David Thoreau, "Civil Disobedience," *Walden and Civil Disobedience* (New York: Rinehart & Co., 1966), p. 225.

4. Ibid., 225.

5. Sinclair, *John Ford*, 110, 114.

6. Bogdanovich, *John Ford*, 86.

7. Ibid.

8. Ibid.

9. Ibid., 74.

10. Ibid., 87.

Chapter Five

1. James Oliver Robertson, *American Myth, American Reality* (New York: Hill & Wang, 1980), 159. Also I have applied Robertson's terms to my first cycle and have accepted his concept of industrial heroes.

2. Douglas Gomery, "Mise-en-scène in Ford's *My Darling Clementine*," *Wide Angle* 2:4 (1978):15-19

3. Ibid., 15-16.

4. David F. Coursen, "John Ford's Wilderness: *The Man Who Shot Liberty Valance*," *Sight and Sound* 47:4 (Autumn, 1978): 240.

Chapter Six

1. The basic concepts and terms for my analysis have been adapted from, primarily, Roland Barthes's "An Introduction to the Structural Analysis of Narrative" and Seymour Chatman's "Towards a Theory of Narrative" in *New Literary History* 6:2 (Winter, 1975).

2. Frye, *Anatomy of Criticism*, 193.

3. Ibid., 187.

4. Ibid., 186.

5. Ibid., 187-88.

6. Bazin, *What is Cinema?* I, 38.

Selected Bibliography

1. Books

Anderson, Lindsay. *About John Ford.* London: Plexus, 1981. A reworking, updating, and gap-filling of Anderson's *Sequence* articles. Generously illustrated.

Baxter, John. *The Cinema of John Ford.* New York: A. S. Barnes & Co., 1971. The first book on Ford in English, both misguided and interesting.

Bogdanovich, Peter. *John Ford.* Berkeley: University of California Press, 1978, rev. ed. The classic film-by-film interview with Ford, including a definitive filmography.

Ford, Dan. *Pappy: The Life of John Ford.* Englewood Cliffs, N. J.: Prentice Hall, 1979. This is as close to an authoritative biography as we are likely to get.

French, Warren. *Filmguide to "The Grapes of Wrath."* Bloomington: Indiana University Press, 1973. A detailed analysis of the novel and the film.

Haudiquet, Phillippe. *John Ford.* Paris: Editions Seghers, 1966. An extremely interesting work on Ford.

McBride, Joseph, and Wilmington, Michael. *John Ford.* London: Secker and Warburg, 1975. First book in English to perform close analysis. There are some excellent essays: *The Quiet Man, The Searchers.*

Mitry, Jean. *John Ford.* Paris: Editions Universitaires, 1954. The first work on Ford is still a classic.

Place, J. A. *The Western Films of John Ford.* Secaucus, N. J.: Citadel Press, 1973. A film-by-film analysis. A thorough work with many stills.

———. *The Non-Western Films of John Ford.* Secaucus, N. J.: Citadel Press, 1979. A film-by-film analysis which divides Ford's films into "genres." It is a thorough work with many stills.

Sarris, Andrew. *The John Ford Movie Mystery.* Bloomington: Indiana University Press, 1975. A brief, insightful, and chronological run through Ford's films.

Sinclair, Andrew. *John Ford.* New York: Dial Press/James Wade, 1979. A biography with critical analyses of the films. There is some interesting biographical information, particularly on the war years, but too much is speculation and the analyses of films are thin.

2. Parts of Books

Anderson, Lindsay. "The Method of John Ford." In *The Emergence of Film Art*, edited by Lewis Jacobs. 2d ed., 230-45. New York: W. W. Norton,

1979. The first in a series of articles on Ford by Anderson who was the editor of the English film magazine, *Sequence*. This essay represents the beginning of critical attention paid to Ford's postwar films. This essay focused on *They Were Expendable*.

Bazin, André. "The Western: Or the American Film Par Excellence" and "The Evolution of the Western." In *What is Cinema? II*, 140-48, 149-57. Berkeley: University of California Press, 1971. Bazin argues that *Stagecoach* is *the* classical Western. He also believes that later Westerns are simply "baroque embellishments" of *Stagecoach*.

Caughie, John, ed. *Theories of Authorship*. London: Routledge & Kegan Paul, 1981. Excellent series of theoretical articles on auteurism with Ford as the central example.

Eisenstein, Sergei. "Mr. Lincoln by Mr. Ford" in *Film-Essays*, edited by Jay Leyda, 139-49. New York: Praeger, 1970. Eisenstein believes *Young Mr. Lincoln* is the American film he would most like to have made. He admires its harmony.

Kaminsky, Stuart M. "The Genre Director: Character Types in the Films of John Ford." In *American Film Genres*, 252-63. New York: Dell, 1977. Kaminsky argues that Ford's characters are archetypal, drawn from popular culture and the Bible.

Lehman, Peter, and Luhr, William. *Authorship and Narrative in the Cinema*, 45-169. New York: G. P. Putnam's Sons, 1977. Half of this book is devoted to Ford, with long detailed chapters on *The Man Who Shot Liberty Valance* and *The Searchers* with good insights, particularly on *The Searchers*.

McConnell, Frank "The Romance World: Knights." In *Storytelling and Mythmaking: Images from Film and Literature*, 83-137. New York: Oxford University Press, 1979. The concepts of medieval romance are applied to film. An analysis of *My Darling Clementine*.

Pechter, William S. "A Persistance of Vision." In *Twenty-Four Times a Second*. New York: Harper & Row, 1971, 226-41. Pechter stresses the thematic unity of Ford's films in a wide-ranging essay.

Thomas, Bob, ed. "John Ford and *Stagecoach*." In *Directors in Action*. New York: Bobb Merrill, 1973, 133-73. Interviews, reminiscences, and articles by Andrew Sarris and Arthur Knight are collected in a valuable inside view.

Wollen, Peter. *Signs and Meaning in the Cinema*. London: Secker & Warburg, 1969, 94-102. An important work in film studies. A section devoted to Ford's mediators and antinomies.

3. Periodicals

Bogdanovich, Peter. "The Cowboy Hero and the American West . . . as Directed by John Ford." *Esquire*, December 1983, 417-25. An overview of Ford's life and films, with special emphasis on the Westerns, John Wayne, and Henry Fonda.

Brewster, Ben. "Notes on the Text 'John Ford's *Young Mr. Lincoln*' by the Editors of *Cahiers du Cinéma*." *Screen*, 14:3 (Autumn 1973):29-43. Brewster argues for a Metzian reading of *Young Mr. Lincoln* without disagreeing with the Cahiers editors.

Browne, Nick. "The Spectator-in-the-Text: The Rhetoric of *Stagecoach*." *Film*

Quarterly 29:2 (Winter, 1975-76): 26-38. This is a very detailed analysis of Ford's point-of-view techniques in the noon-meal scene of *Stagecoach.*

Campbell, Russell. "*Fort Apache*," *Velvet Light Trap* (Summer, 1971), 8-12. This an early analysis of Ford's style and themes in one of the Cavalry Trilogy films.

Coursen, David. "John Ford Reprints the Legend," *Movietone News* 42 (2 July, 1975): 3-11. This is a penetrating comparison of *Judge Priest* and *The Sun Shines Bright.* Coursen stresses their differences, making a strong case for the complexity of the later Ford films.

————. "John Ford: Assessing the Reassessment." *Film Quarterly* 29:3 (Spring, 1976):58-60. This is a critical reply to the Michael Dempsey "reassessment" of the "myth of Ford's great artistry."

————. "John Ford's Wilderness: *The Man Who Shot Liberty Valance*." *Sight and Sound* 47:4 (Autumn, 1978): 237-41. Coursen argues convincingly for Ford's ambivalence regarding the wilderness and the garden, the past and the present.

Dempsey, Michael. "John Ford: A Reassessment." *Film Quarterly* 28:4 (Summer, 1975):2-15. Dempsey attacks Ford's "emotional facility . . . weak-kneed liberalism . . . paternalism," and treatments of minorities and women.

Editors, *Cahiers du Cinéma*. "John Ford's *Young Mr. Lincoln*." *Screen* 13:3 (Autumn, 1972):5-44. The monumental collective analyses by the editors of *Cahiers du Cinéma* No. 223 (1970), translated into English by Helen Lackner and Diana Matias. Also reprinted in *Movies and Methods*, edited by Bill Nichols (Berkeley, University of California Press, 1976) and *Film Theory and Criticism*, 2d ed., edited by Gerald Mast and Marshall Cohen. This essay is one of the great works of modern film criticism. It spawned many responses, including a short afterword by Peter Wollen in the *Screen* issue.

Editors, *Movietone News*. "John Ford (1895-1973)." *Movietown News* 26 (October, 1973), unpaginated center section. An evocative remembrance of Ford's private moments. This is essentially a pictorial and written poem devoted to Ford's special epiphanies.

Editors, *Screen Education*. "Special Issue on Teaching *The Searchers*." *Screen Education* 17 (Autumn, 1975):1-57. Semiotic approaches are applied to *The Searchers* with mixed success by John Caughie, David Lusted, Tom Ryall, Douglas Pye, Edward Buscombe, Alan Lovell.

Ellis, Kirk. "On the Warpath: John Ford and the Indians." *Journal of Popular Film and Television* 8:2 (1980): 34-41. The only accurate and carefully argued defense of Ford's portrayal of Indians.

Fleischer, Stefan. "A Study Through Stills of *My Darling Clementine*." *Journal of Modern Literature* 3:2 (April, 1973):241-52.

Greenfield, Pierre. "Print the Fact: For and Against the Films of John Ford." *Take One* 12:5 (November, 1977): 15-19. He attacks Ford's "gross pandering to bourgeois complacency . . . innate conformism." Ford is also naive, simplistic, and jingoistic. Greenfield then lamely describes Ford's strengths.

Henderson, Brian. "Critique of Cine-Structuralism, Part II." *Film Quarterly*

27:2 (Winter, 1973-74). Reprinted in *A Critique of Film Theory* by Henderson. New York: E. P. Dutton, 1980, 218-33. Henderson argues that the *Cahiers* essay is an active reading of the text, while Ben Brewster's is a confused, object-oriented, Metzian reading.

Lehman, Peter, ed. "Special John Ford Issue." *Wide Angle* 2:4 (1978): 2-61. An uneven collection of articles. The best are by Lehman on offscreen space and by Douglas Gomery on the civilization iconography of *My Darling Clementine*.

Nichols, Bill. "Style, Grammar, and the Movies." *Film Quarterly* 28:3 (Spring, 1975): 33-49. Reprinted in *Movies and Methods*, edited by Bill Nichols (Berkeley, University of California Press, 1976). "The ultimate goal of the orientation begun here is to bring about a merger of Freud and Marx—the personal and the political, the 'languange of the unconscious' and the structure of society—to link up visual/formal analysis with scientific, ideological analysis." He applies this methodology to *Young Mr. Lincoln* and *My Darling Clementine*.

Nowell-Smith, Geoffrey. "Six Authors in Pursuit of *The Searchers*." *Screen* 17:1 (Spring, 1976):26-33. Nowell-Smith argues that that *Screen Education* issue devoted to *The Searchers* is ultimately auteurist even though its ideological stance is anti-auteurist.

Rohdie, Sam. "Who Shot Liberty Valance?" *Salmagundi* 29 (Spring, 1975): 159-71. A structural analysis of the narrative significance of lying in *Fort Apache* and *The Man Who Shot Liberty Valance*.

Rubin, Martin. "Mr. Ford and Mr. Rogers: The Will Rogers Trilogy." *Film Comment* 10:1 (January-February, 1974): 54-57. Rubin argues that it is the "light" Will Rogers trilogy rather than the "dark" *Informer* and *Lost Patrol* that "represent his most important developments in theme ai.d tone of the middle thirties."

Silver, Charles. "The Apprenticeship of John Ford." *American Film* 1 (May, 1976):62-67. This is an early look at the Museum of Modern Art's collection of Ford's extant silent films.

Wood, Robin. "Shall We Gather at the River? The Late Films of John Ford." *Film Comment* 7 (Fall, 1971):8-17. Wood convincingly argues that Ford's late films, *Donovan's Reef, Cheyenne Autumn,* and *7 Women* are not the great masterpieces that overzealous Ford enthusiasts make them out to be.

Selected Filmography

DR. BULL (Fox, 1933)
Screenplay: Paul Green, from novel, *The Last Adam,* by James Gould
Cozzens
Dialogue: Jane Storm
Cinematographer: George Schneiderman
Music: Samuel Kaylin
Cast: Will Rogers (Dr. Bull), Marian Nixon (May Tripping), Berton Churchill
(Herbert Banning), Louise Dresser (Mrs. Banning), Howard Lally (Joe
Tripping), Rochelle Hudson (Virginia Banning), Vera Allen (Janet Carmaker),
Andy Devine (Larry Ward), Robert Parrish, Si Jenks
Running time: 76 minutes
Release date: 22 September 1933, Radio City Music Hall,
New York City
16mm rental: Films Inc.

JUDGE PRIEST (Fox, 1934)
Producer: Sol Wurtzel
Screenplay: Dudley Nichols, Lamar Trotti, from stories by Irvin S. Cobb
Cinematographer: George Schneiderman
Music: Samuel Kaylin
Cast: Will Rogers (Judge William "Billy" Priest), Henry B. Walthall
(Reverend Ashby Brand), Tom Brown (Jerome Priest), Anita Louise (Ellie
May Gillespie), Rochelle Hudson (Virginia Maydew), Berton Churchill
(Senator Horace K. Maydew), David Landau (Bob Gillis), Brenda Fowler
(Mrs. Caroline Priest), Hattie McDaniel (Aunt Delsey), Stepin Fetchit (Jeff
Poindexter), Roger Imhof, Charley Grapewin, Francis Ford, Louis Mason,
Robert Parrish
Running Time: 80 minutes
Release date: 5 October 1934, Radio City Music Hall, New York City
16mm rental: Films Inc., Budget Films, Kit Parker Films (longest version)

STEAMBOAT ROUND THE BEND (Twentieth Century-Fox, 1935)
Producer: Sol M. Wurtzel
Assistant director: Edward O'Fearna (Ford's brother)
Screenplay: Dudley Nichols, Lamar Trotti, from story by Ben Lucien
Burman

Cinematographer: George Schneiderman
Art director: William Darling
Set decorator: Albert Hogsett
Music director: Samuel Kaylin
Editor: Alfred De Gaetano
Cast: Will Rogers (Dr. John Pearly), Anne Shirley (Fleety Belle), Eugene Pallette (Sheriff Rufe Jeffers), John McGuire (Duke), Berton Churchill (the New Moses), Stepin Fetchit (George Lincoln Washington), Francis Ford (Efe), Irvin S. Cobb (Captain Eli), Roger Imhof (Pappy), Louis Mason (boat race organizer), Si Jenks (a drunk), Jack Pennick (ringleader of boat attack)
Running time: 80 minutes
Release date: 6 September 1935, Radio City Music Hall,
New York City
16mm rental: Films Inc.

STAGECOACH (Wanger–United Artists, 1939)
Executive producer: Walter Wanger
Assistant director: Wingate Smith
Screenplay: Dudley Nichols, from story, "Stage to Lordsburg," by Ernest Haycox
Cinematographer: Bert Glennon
Art director: Alexander Toluboff
Set decorator: Wiard B. Ihnen
Costumes: Walter Plunkett
Music: Richard Hageman, W. Franke Harling, John Leipold, Leo Shuken, Louis Grueberg (adapted from seventeen American folk tunes of the early 1880s)
Editorial supervisor: Otho Lovering
Editors: Dorothy Spencer, Walter Reynolds
Cast: John Wayne (the Ringo Kid), Claire Trevor (Dallas), John Carradine (Hatfield), Thomas Mitchell (Dr. Josiah Boone), Andy Devine (Buck), Donald Meek (Samuel Peacock), Louise Platt (Lucy Mallory), Tim Holt (Lieutenant Blanchard), George Bancroft (Sheriff Curly Wilcox), Berton Churchill (Henry Gatewood), Francis Ford, Yakima Canutt, Chief Big Tree, Jack Pennick, Louis Mason, Vester Pegg
Running time: 97 minutes
Release date: 2 March 1939, Radio City Music Hall, New York City
16mm rental: Films Inc., Audio Brandon, Kit Parker Films, Budget Films

YOUNG MR. LINCOLN (Cosmopolitan–Twentieth Century-Fox, 1939)
Executive producer: Darryl F. Zanuck
Producer: Kenneth Macgowan
Screenplay: Lamar Trotti, based on the life of Abraham Lincoln
Cinematographer: Bert Glennon
Art directors: Richard Day, Mark Lee Kirk
Set decorator: Thomas Little
Music: Alfred Newman
Editor: Walter Thompson

Sound effects editor: Robert Parrish
Cast: Henry Fonda (Abraham Lincoln), Alice Brady (Abigail Clay), Marjorie
Weaver (Mary Todd), Arleen Whelan (Hannah Clay), Eddie Collins (Efe
Turner), Pauline Moore (Ann Rutledge), Ward Bond (John Palmer Cass),
Donald Meek (John Felder), Francis Ford, Russell Simpson, Louis Mason,
Jack Pennick
Running time: 101 minutes
Release date: 2 June 1939, Roxy Theatre, New York City
16mm rental: Films Inc.

DRUMS ALONG THE MOHAWK (Twentieth Century-Fox, 1939)
Executive producer: Darryl F. Zanuck
Producer: Raymond Griffith
Screenplay: Lamar Trotti, Sonya Levien, from novel by Walter D. Edmonds
Cinematographers: (in Technicolor) Bert Glennon, Ray Rennahan
Art directors: Richard Day, Mark Lee Kirk
Set decorator: Thomas Little
Music: Alfred Newman
Editor: Robert Simpson
Sound effects editor: Robert Parrish
Cast: Claudette Colbert (Lana Borst Martin), Henry Fonda (Gilbert Martin),
Edna May Oliver (Mrs. McKlennar), Eddie Collins (Christian Reall), John
Carradine (Caldwell), Arthur Shields (Father Rosenkranz), Roger Imhof
(General Nicholas Herkimer), Francis Ford (Joe Boleo), Ward Bond (Adam
Hartmann), Russell Simpson (Dr. Petry), Chief Big Tree (Blue Back), Si
Jenks, Jack Pennick, Mae Marsh
Running time: 103 minutes
Release date: 3 November 1939, Roxy Theatre, New York City
16mm rental: Films Inc.

THE GRAPES OF WRATH (Twentieth Century-Fox, 1940)
Producer: Darryl F. Zanuck
Associate producer: Nunnally Johnson
Assistant director: Edward O'Fearna (Ford's brother)
Screenplay: Nunnally Johnson, from novel by John Steinbeck
Cinematographer: Gregg Toland
Art directors: Richard Day, Mark Lee Kirk
Set decorator: Thomas Little
Music: Alfred Newman (song, "Red River Valley," played on accordion by
Dan Borzage)
Editor: Robert Simpson
Sound: George Leverett, Roger Heman
Sound effects editor: Robert Parrish
Cast: Henry Fonda (Tom Joad), Jane Darwell (Ma Joad), John Carradine
(Casy), Charley Grapewin (Grampa Joad), Russell Simpson (Pa Joad), John
Qualen (Muley), Zeffie Tilbury (Grandma Joad), Grant Mitchell (Camp
director), Ward Bond, Joe Sawyer, Roger Imhof, Mae Marsh, Francis Ford,
Jack Pennick, Louis Mason
Running time: 129 minutes

Release date: 24 January 1940, Rivoli Theatre, New York City
16mm rental: Films Inc.

TOBACCO ROAD (Twentieth Century-Fox, 1941)
Producer: Darryl F. Zanuck
Associated producers: Jack Kirkland, Harry H. Oshrin
Screenplay: Nunnally Johnson, from play by Kirkland and novel by Erskine Caldwell
Cinematographer: Arthur C. Miller
Art directors: Richard Day, James Basevi
Set decorator: Thomas Little
Music: David Buttolph
Editor: Barbara McLean
Sound effects editor: Robert Parrish
Cast: Charley Grapewin (Jeeter Lester), Marjorie Rambeau (Sister Bessie), Gene Tierney (Ellie May Lester), William Tracy (Dude Lester), Elizabeth Patterson (Ada Lester), Dana Andrews (Captain Tim), Slim Summerville (Henry Peabody), Ward Bond (Lov Bensey), Grant Mitchell (George Payne), Zeffie Tilbury (Grandma Lester), Russell Simpson, Jack Pennick, Francis Ford
Running time: 84 minutes
Release date: 20 February 1941, Roxy Theatre, New York City
16mm rental: Films Inc., Audio Brandon, Budget Films

MY DARLING CLEMENTINE (Twentieth Century-Fox, 1946)
Producer: Samuel G. Engel
Assistant director: William Eckhardt
Screenplay: Samuel G. Engel, Winston Miller, from story by Sam Hellman, based on book, *Wyatt Earp, Frontier Marshal* by Stuart N. Lake
Cinematographer: Joseph P MacDonald
Art directors: James Basevi, Lyle R. Wheeler
Set decorators: Thomas Little, Fred J. Rode
Costumes: Rene Hubert
Music: Cyril J. Mockridge
Editor: Dorothy Spencer
Cast: Henry Fonda (Wyatt Earp), Linda Darnell (Chihuahua), Victor Mature (Doc John Holliday), Walter Brennan (Old Man Clanton), Tim Holt (Virgil Earp), Ward Bond (Morgan Earp), Cathy Downs (Clementine Carter), Alan Mowbray (Granville Thorndyke), John Ireland (Billy Clanton), Russell Simpson, Francis Ford, J. Farrell McDonald, Arthur Walsh, Jack Pennick, Mae Marsh
Running time: 97 minutes
Release date: 3 December 1946, Rivoli Theatre, New York City
16mm rental: Films Inc.

FORT APACHE (Argosy Pictures–RKO Radio, 1948)
Producers: John Ford, Merian C. Cooper
Production manager: Bernard McEveety
Assistant directors: Lowell Farrell, Jack Pennick

Second-unit director: Cliff Lyons
Screenplay: Frank S. Nugent, from story, "Massacre," by James Warner
Bellah
Cinematographer: Archie Stout
Art director: James Basevi
Set decorator: Joe Kish
Music: Richard Hageman
Cast: Henry Fonda (Lieutenant Colonel Owen Thursday), Shirley Temple
(Philadelphia Thursday), John Agar (Lieutenant Michael O'Rourke), Ward
Bond (Sergeant Major O'Rourke). George O'Brien (Captain Sam
Collingwood), Victor McLaglen (Sergeant Mulcahy), Pedro Armendariz,
Anna Lee, Guy Kibbee, Jack Pennick, Mae Marsh, Francis Ford, Hank
Worden
Running time: 127 minutes
Release date: 9 March 1948 (24 June 1948, Capitol Theatre, New York City)
16mm rental: Audio Brandon

SHE WORE A YELLOW RIBBON (Argosy Pictures–RKO Radio, 1949)
Producers: John Ford, Merian C. Cooper
Associate producer: Lowell Farrell
Assistant directors: Wingate Smith, Edward O'Fearna (Ford's brother)
Second-unit director: Cliff Lyons
Screenplay: Frank S. Nugent, Laurence Stallings, from story, "War Party,"
by James Warner Bellah
Cinematographers: (in Technicolor) Winton C. Hoch, Charles P. Boyle
(second-unit)
Art director: James Basevi
Set decorator: Joe Kish
Music: Richard Hageman
Editor: Jack Murray
Assistant editor: Barbara Ford (Ford's daughter)
Cast: John Wayne (Captain Nathan Brittles), Joanne Dru (Olivia), John Agar
(Lieutenant Flint Cohil), Ben Johnson (Sergeant Tyree), Harry Carey, Jr.
(Lieutenant Pennell), Victor McLaglen (Sergeant Quincannon), Mildred
Natwick (Mrs. Allshard), George O'Brien (Major Allshard), Arthur Shields,
Francis Ford, Chief Big Tree, Jack Pennick
Running time: 103 minutes
Release date: 22 October 1949 (17 November 1949, Capitol Theatre, New
York City)
16mm rental: Audio Brandon, Budget Films

RIO GRANDE (Argosy Pictures–Republic, 1950)
Producers: John Ford, Merian C. Cooper
Second-unit director: Cliff Lyons
Screenplay: James Kevin McGuinness, from story, "Mission With No
Record," by James Warner Bellah
Cinematographers: Bert Glennon, Archie Stout (second-unit)
Art director: Frank Hotaling

Set decorators: John McCarthy, Jr., Charles Thompson
Costumes: Adele Palmer
Music: Victor Young
Editor: Jack Murray
Assistant editor: Barbara Ford (Ford's daughter)
Cast: John Wayne (Lieutenant Colonel Kirby Yorke), Maureen O'Hara (Mrs. Kathleen Yorke), Ben Johnson (Trooper Tyree), Claude Jarman, Jr. (Trooper Jefferson Yorke), Harry Carey, Jr. (Trooper Daniel Boone), Chill Wills (Dr. Wilkins), J. Carroll Naish (General Philip Sheridan), Victor McLaglen (Sergeant Quincannon), Jack Pennick, Pat Wayne, The Sons of the Pioneers (regimental singers): Ken Curtis, Hugh Farr, Karl Farr, Lloyd Perryman, Shug Fisher, Tommy Doss
Running time: 105 minutes
Release date: 15 November 1950, Mayfair Theater, New York City
16mm rental: Kit Parker Films, Budget Films

THE SEARCHERS (C. V. Whitney Pictures–Warner Bros., 1956)
Producer: C. V. Whitney
Executive producer: Merian C. Cooper
Associate producer: Patrick Ford (Ford's son)
Production supervisor: Lowell Farrell
Assistant director: Wingate Smith
Screenplay: Frank S. Nugent, from novel by Alan LeMay
Cinematographers: (in Technicolor and VistaVision) Winston C. Hoch, Alfred Gilks (second-unit)
Art directors: Frank Hotaling, James Basevi
Set decorator: Victor Gangelin
Music: Max Steiner
Editor: Jack Murray
Cast: John Wayne (Ethan Edwards), Jeffrey Hunter (Martin Pawley), Vera Miles (Laurie Jorgensen), Ward Bond (Captain/Reverend Samuel Clayton), Natalie Wood (Debbie Edwards), John Qualen (Lars Jorgensen), Olive Carey (Mrs. Jorgensen), Henry Brandon (Chief Scar), Ken Curtis (Charlie McCorry), Harry Carey, Jr. (Brad Jorgensen), Hank Worden (Mose Harper), Pat Wayne, Jack Pennick, Mae Marsh, Dan Borzage
Running time: 119 minutes
Release date: 26 May 1956, Criterion Theater, New York City
16mm rental: Swank Motion Pictures

THE MAN WHO SHOT LIBERTY VALANCE (Ford Productions–Paramount, 1962)
Producer: Willis Goldbeck
Assistant director: Wingate Smith
Screenplay: Willis Goldbeck, James Warner Bellah, from story by Dorothy M. Johnson
Cinematographer: William H. Clothier
Art directors: Hal Perira, Eddie Imazu
Set decorators: Sam Comer, Darrell Silvera

Costumes: Edith Head
Music: Cyril J. Mockridge
Editor: Otho Lovering
Cast: James Stewart (Ransom Stoddard), John Wayne (Tom Doniphon), Vera
Miles (Hallie Stoddard), Lee Marvin (Liberty Valance), Edmond O'Brien
(Dutton Peabody), Andy Devine (Link Appleyard), Ken Murray (Doc
Willoughby), John Carradine (Starbuckle), Jeanette Nolan (Nora Ericson),
John Qualen (Peter Ericson), Willis Bouchey, Carleton Young, Woody
Strode, Strother Martin, Lee Van Cleef, O. Z. Whitehead, Jack Pennick,
Anna Lee, Shug Fisher
Running time: 122 minutes
Release date: April 1962 (23 May 1962, Capitol Theatre, New York City)
16mm rental: Audio Brandon

Index